ESSEX COUNT

CLU

An A–Z

*Wicketkeeper David East took eight catches out
of the nine Somerset wickets to fall at
Taunton in 1985.*

Dean Hayes

For my son, Ben, who thankfully
shares my love of the game

First published in 2001 by S. B. Publications,
19 Grove Road, Seaford, East Sussex BN25 1TP

ISBN 1 85770 228 X

Designed and typeset by CGB, Lewes
Printed by MFP Design and Print
Longford Trading Estate, Thomas Street,
Stretford, Manchester M32 0JT

ABOUT THE AUTHOR

Dean Hayes is an experienced freelance sports writer specialising in football and cricket. He was educated at Hayward Grammar School, Bolton and West Midlands College of Physical Education and was a Primary School Head Teacher until taking up writing on a permanent basis five years ago.

He has played football in the Lancashire Amateur League, but he now concentrates solely on playing the summer game. This former cricket professional, now playing as an amateur, has taken well over 2,000 wickets in league cricket.

Dean is married to Elaine and has one son and two stepchildren. This is his eleventh book on cricket to be published – a twelfth on Kent CCC is in course of preparation – and his fifty-sixth overall.

Front cover: Clockwise from top left: Graham Gooch, Jack O'Connor, Nasser Hussain, Stan Nichols, A C Smith, Peter Smith..

ACKNOWLEDGEMENTS

The author wishes to thank the following organisations for their help in compiling this book: Essex County Cricket Club, The British Newspaper Library and the Association of Cricket Statisticians.

Thanks also to the following individuals: Ben Hayes, Peter Stafford and Steve Benz for publishing the first in a series of County Cricket Club A–Zs.

PICTURE CREDITS

The illustrations in the book were kindly provided by the *Lancashire Evening Post* – with others from the author's personal collection.

SELECT BIBLIOGRAPHY

Bailey, Trevor. *Championship Cricket.* Frederick Muller 1961
Bray, Charles. *Essex County Cricket.* Convoy Publications 1950
Essex County Cricket Handbooks 1980-2000
Lemmon, D and Marshall, M. *Essex County Cricket Club – The Official History* 1987
Newnham, Leslie. *Essex County Cricket 1876-1975*

A

ACFIELD, DAVID

David Acfield, a Cambridge undergraduate from Brentwood School, took six for 69 for the University against Essex before making his county debut in 1966. He also gained recognition at international level for England as a fencer, appearing in the Olympic Games and winning a gold medal at the Commonwealth Games in Edinburgh.He was also the British Sabre Champion.

David Acfield.

When Robin Hobbs left for Glamorgan in 1975, it allowed Acfield more chances. He responded with consistent, effective bowling performances. He took four for 96 and seven for 57 against Surrey at the Oval in 1976, also representing the MCC against the West Indies. It was the second time he had represented the MCC, having played against the champion county, Hampshire, in 1974.

Acfield's most successful season was 1981 when he headed the county's bowling averages with 76 wickets at 22.61 runs apiece. During the course of the summer, he returned the best figures of his career, eight for 55 against Kent at Canterbury.

The county's first championship victory of 1983 brought about a remarkable bowling performance from David Acfield. Essex's opponents were Somerset – the venue Taunton. Essex totalled 262, Somerset declaring on reaching 250 with Acfield taking four for 106. Essex scored quickly in their second innings and so set the home side a target of 255 to win in three-and-a-half hours. After a cautious start, Acfield took five for one in thirteen balls and ended with six for 34 as Essex won by 141 runs.

As a batsman and often at Number 11, Acfield turned in quite a few performances of great resolution which were the margin between defeat and victory, though his top score for Essex was only 38 made against Nottinghamshire at Chelmsford in 1973.

If he had played in the 1950s or 1960s Acfield, who took 855 wickets at 27.49, would have had far greater opportunity to bowl his off-spin. Instead, for much of his career, this underrated bowler, had to contend with the great predominance of seam bowlers in the Essex side.

APPEARANCES

The players with the highest number of first-class appearances for Essex are as follows:

1	Keith Fletcher	1962-1989	574
2	Brian Taylor	1949-1973	539
3	Percy Perrin	1896-1928	525
4	Jack O'Connor	1921-1939	516
5	Trevor Bailey	1946-1967	482
6	Johnny Douglas	1901-1928	459
7	Gordon Barker	1954-1971	444
8	Lawrie Eastman	1920-1939	442
9	John Lever	1967-1989	439
10	Peter Smith	1929-1951	434

Graham Gooch has appeared in a total of 821 matches for Essex. This comprises of 375 first-class games, 274 Sunday League games, 115 Benson and Hedges Cup games and 57 Nat West/Gillette games.

AUSTRALIA

The Australian touring side of 1893 had been scheduled to play Cambridge Past and Present at Leyton but as Cambridge found it impossible to put together a side, Essex took over the fixture. The side performed admirably with Walter Mead taking nine for 136 in the first innings and eight for 69 in the second, as Essex earned an honourable draw.

Essex began the 1899 season in sensational style, beating the

Australians at Leyton by 126 runs. After a last wicket partnership of 55 between Young and Lucas, Essex were all out for 199 with Trumble having taken eight for 79. After gaining a first innings lead of 55 runs, Essex were indebted to Arthur Turner with 54 as they were bowled out for 144, leaving Australia to score 200 for victory. Sailor Young who took seven wickets and had match figures of 11 for 74, and bowling unchanged with Mead, helped dismiss the Australians for 73.

The county recorded another victory over the Australians in 1905. In a low-scoring match, Essex were bowled out for 118 but fine bowling by Buckenham and Tremlin gave the home side a first innings lead of 18. After a better batting display in their second innings, Essex set the tourists 222 to win but they failed to reach their target by 20 runs as Buckenham with match figures of 12 for 137 wrapped things up.

Donald Bradman's 1948 Australians were probably the most formidable combination ever to tour England. They arrived at Southend having won their first five matches, four of them by an innings. Just before the close of the first day, they were all out for 721, the highest total ever scored in a single day's first-class cricket. Essex were bowled out for 83 and although Pearce and Peter Smith showed some resistance in the second innings, the margin of defeat was an innings and 451 runs.

Essex's first victory over the Australians for 59 years came at Southend in August 1964 and was achieved in grand style. Keith Fletcher (125) and Gordon Barker (123) helped Essex reach 425 for six before they declared, despite losing time to the weather. The Australians were bowled out for 218 with Paddy Phelan taking five for 94. Bailey enforced the follow-on and Australia, faring better the second time, scored 313. Needing 107 to win, Essex knocked off the runs for the loss of four wickets.

In the 1975 game at Chelmsford, Robin Hobbs reached his hundred in 44 minutes – in a game played in a carnival atmosphere. It was the fastest hundred by an Essex player and the fastest conceded by any touring team. In spite of all that the Australians won by 98 runs.

AVERY, SONNY

By the age of fifteen, Sonny Avery was an office boy at the Essex club, a job that gave him a perfect view of the playing area. He had been on the ground staff a long time, showing excellent promise, before being given his county debut in 1935 when his perseverance was rewarded.

Avery, who scored his maiden century, 109 against Nottinghamshire at Trent Bridge in 1937, was also a good footballer, playing for Leyton against Dulwich Hamlet in the 1937 FA Amateur Cup Final.

After the Second World War, he continued where he had left off in 1939 and scored a double century in the match against Surrey at the Oval. His score of 210 contained twenty boundaries as he and Dickie Dodds put on 270 in a record breaking opening partnership. In 1948, Avery scored 1,890 runs, including six centuries. His top score was 214 not out in the match against Worcestershire when he and Dick Horsfall put on 298, a record fourth wicket partnership. The following season, Avery scored a century in each innings, 117 and 100 in the match against Glamorgan at Ebbw Vale.

In 1952, Avery topped the Essex batting averages with 1,441 runs at an average of 41.17. It was during this season that he and Paul Gibb set a new record second wicket partnership of 294 against Northamptonshire, Avery going on to hit 224, the highest score of his career. He hit another double hundred the following summer – 208 not out against Glamorgan at Westcliff. In 1954, Avery carried his bat through an innings for the third time but he was hampered by injuries and forced to miss the second half of the season, at the end of which he decided to retire.

Sonny Avery had joined the Essex staff as a left-arm spin bowler but developed into a very good opening batsman, scoring 14,045 runs at 33.60, and playing many correct, yet stylish, innings.

BAILEY, TREVOR

Trevor Bailey played his first games for Essex during the war years, impressing immediately in his opening game with four for 36 including three wickets in his first over. He also represented several sides at Lord's including an England XI against a West Indian XI and the British Empire XI when on leave from the Royal Marines.

After the war, Bailey attended Cambridge University and was only able to appear for Essex at the end of term. However, in only his second season, he hit a superb 205 against Sussex at Eastbourne – it was to be his highest score in first-class cricket.

Throughout the cricketing world, Trevor Bailey is 'The Boil'. This unusual nickname originated from a visit to Switzerland in the winter of 1947-48 with the Cambridge University soccer team. The Swiss announcer was having difficulty with the longer names in the Cambridge XI and announced that 'Boiley' would play at outside-right. This was subsequently abbreviated to 'The Boil' and its adoption by Freddie Brown on the Australian tour of 1950-51 ensured its permanency.

At the beginning of the 1948 season, it was decided to offer Bailey the position of assistant-secretary, thus enabling him to devote his full time to playing first-class cricket after coming down from Cambridge. Thankfully he accepted.

In 1949, every possible distinction came to Trevor Bailey. He was selected by the MCC for its match against New Zealand and followed it by playing in four successive Test matches. During this four match series, he had scores of 93 and 72 not out and bowling figures of six for 84 and six for 118 – which he took in his first Test. He achieved the double, scoring 1,380 runs and capturing 130 wickets, and in the match against Lancashire at Clacton took all ten wickets in the red rose county's first innings for 90 runs. He thus became only the second Essex bowler to accomplish this feat, the other being Henry Pickett. Not surprisingly, he was chosen as one of *Wisden's* Five Cricketers of the Year. In 1950, he took seven for nought in thirty-one balls against Glamorgan at Brentwood and in the return match at Newport, recorded a hat-trick.

When injuries began to restrict his appearances for Essex, he managed to gain an FA Amateur Cup Winners' medal while playing for Walthamstow Avenue against Leyton.

In 1953 he was appointed Essex's vice-captain, a position he was to hold until he took over as captain from Doug Insole. During the Test series against Australia, his innings of 71 in the fifth wicket partnership of 163 with Willie Watson saved the series for England. In the winter tour to the West Indies, he turned in his best bowling figures in Test cricket, taking seven for 34 at Kingston.

He had the reputation for some dour performances with the bat, Neville Cardus saying that he 'stonewalled with passion'. In 1955 he hit a hundred before lunch against Nottinghamshire at Southend and over the next couple of seasons, topped both the county's batting and bowling averages. In 1957 in the Lord's Test match against the West Indies, he took seven for 44 in twenty-one overs. It was his fiftieth Test match and his victims included Walcott, Weekes and Worrell. Bailey represented his country on sixty-one occasions, scoring 2,290 runs and capturing 132 wickets.

In 1959, Bailey scored 2,011 runs and took 100 wickets. It was the first time such a feat had been performed by an Essex player. Bailey began the 1961 season as Essex captain, a natural successor to Doug Insole, who had resigned owing to business commitments. He led by example. He achieved the double for the seventh time and repeated the feat in the following season but injuries then restricted his appearances and in 1967, after scoring 21,460 runs and taking 1,593 wickets, he decided to retire – a quite irreparable loss to Essex cricket.

Trevor Bailey, without doubt the finest all-round cricketer ever to play for Essex, went on to become an important member of BBC radio's cricket commentary team.

BARKER, GORDON

Gordon Barker learnt much of his early cricket in the tough Bradford League with other players like Ray Illingworth and Doug Padgett. While completing his National Service, he represented the Army at cricket, hitting a century against the Navy and 67 not out against the RAF. His two years in the forces gave him the opportunity to play in a class of cricket above that which he had previously experienced. He was discovered playing in a match at Richmond by Doug Insole and Trevor Bailey and was given a trial by Essex. He made a dismal start against the touring Canadians, being dismissed for nought but came back strongly in the second innings with 107 not out.

In his first full season of county championship cricket in 1955, Barker scored 1,494 runs and was immediately awarded his county cap. He scored his runs very quickly and proved to be the ideal opening partner for Dickie Dodds, the pair of them once rattling up 159 before lunch against Kent at Clacton in 1957.

Soccer too was a strong interest for several years and he played on the wing for five seasons with Southend United at Roots Hall in the Third Division, followed by spells with both Chelmsford and Romford.

Barker, who scored 1,000 runs in a season on fifteen occasions, settled into another successful opening partnership, this time with Geoffrey Smith, following the departure of Dickie Dodds. In 1961, he made the highest score of his career – 181 not out against Kent at Colchester which included getting to his hundred before lunch. By 1964, Barker had formed a third successful opening partnership with Michael Bear. Now a senior professional in the Essex side, he did on occasions lead the club in Bailey's absence.

He showed too that he could adapt to one-day cricket and in 1971, his last season in first-class cricket, he topped the national averages in the John Player League with 449 runs at 56.12.

Gordon Barker was the mainstay of the Essex batting line-up for many years, scoring 21,895 runs. On his retirement from first-class cricket, he became cricket coach at Felsted, producing such outstanding players as Derek Pringle and John Stephenson.

BEAR, MICHAEL

Brentwood-born batsman Michael Bear joined Essex in 1954, making his maiden century against Gloucestershire at Romford in 1957. However, halfway through the following summer he lost his form and was demoted to the 2nd XI, yet he had scored 913 runs in the matches he had played in and was awarded his county cap.

Bear soon earned a reputation as a fielder who picked up and threw in all in one movement. His superb work in the field was talked about throughout the land. In 1962 he was switched to opening the innings for Essex. The move worked well for Bear had his most successful season, scoring 1,612 runs at 29.85 including two centuries.

The following season he broke his leg when, with six games to play, he had scored 1,170 runs at an average of 30.00. In 1964, Bear continued to bat well when other Essex players were struggling to find their form, scoring 1,567 runs at an average of 29.56. In the match against Gloucestershire at Bristol, Essex were chasing 181 to win in two-and-a-hours. They won the game by six wickets with just two minutes to spare, Bear hitting a quick-fire unbeaten 81. After a disappointing season in 1965, Bear was back to his best the following summer, topping the Essex batting averages with 1,883 runs at 32.15.

A more than useful county cricketer, Michael Bear scored 12,564 runs and topped 1,000 runs in four seasons but he had to retire at the end of the 1968 season due to injury.

BENSON AND HEDGES CUP

Essex has been involved in six Benson and Hedges Cup Finals. Its success in beating Surrey by 35 runs in 1979, was the first honour of any kind which the county had won since its formation in 1876. When Essex were 172 for one, it looked as if they were almost home and dry but although they scored 290 for six, an almost unassailable total in a 55-over game, Surrey made a brave fight of it. Graham Gooch, who was voted Man-of-the-Match, scored 120 in an innings of fluent stroke play and he was well supported by Ken McEwan, who made 72. At 45 for two, Surrey looked on the way out but Howarth and Knight pulled the innings together and at 136 for two, Surrey were still in the hunt. However, wickets had to be surrendered in the chase for runs and after the tail was brushed aside, Essex had tasted success at last after more than 100 years of trying.

Essex returned to Lord's the following season in the hope of becoming the first county to win successively. Their opponents were Northamptonshire who found batting rather difficult except, that is, for Allan Lamb, whose brilliant 72 gave the innings the character it would have lacked without it. They were all out for 209 and with Essex on 112 for one and Graham Gooch and Ken McEwan in full flow, victory for the side batting second seemed assured. But in a flash, 112 for one became 129 for five. Norbert Phillip nearly swung the game round and was still unbeaten on 32 when Essex ran out of overs with two wickets still standing and just six runs needed for victory. If they still had a wicket in hand, it could have been an absorbing situation had there been just one more over.

Although Middlesex won the 1983 Benson and Hedges Final, there is no doubt that Essex threw it away. Fletcher put Middlesex into bat and with Radley scoring 89, they finished on 196 for eight. Essex were 127 for one and sailing home but then panic set in and wickets began to fall. In fact, Essex went into full retreat – run outs, a catch by a substitute fielder and so it was all finally poised for the last over. Five to win and Essex reduced to their last line of defence – Foster and Lever. Sadly, one ball was enough as Cowans bowled Neil Foster.

Essex's next appearance in the Benson and Hedges final was in 1985 when their opponents were Leicestershire. Not surprisingly, in what was one of the wettest of summers, the pitch was sluggish and made for a dour and predictable match until Leicestershire's Peter Willey guided his side to victory. Psychologically, Essex never atoned for the loss of both their injured captain and the toss. Graham Gooch, however, led the side most ably, top-scoring with 57 in an Essex total of 213 for eight. He even temporarily recovered the initiative for Essex with a dramatic spell of swing bowling which claimed two wickets for just five runs in fourteen balls and earned him the accolade of an umpire's warning for damaging the pitch. Willey's 86 helped Leicestershire win by five wickets and in doing so, they recorded the highest total to win this final for a team batting second.

Essex's fifth appearance in the Benson and Hedges final was in 1989 when their opponents were Nottinghamshire. Essex batted first and scored 243 for seven in their 55-overs with Alan Lilley finishing on 95 not out. John Lever got Essex's bowling off to a dream start, removing both Nottinghamshire openers with just 17 on the board. Robinson and

Johnson then put on 132 runs before wickets began to tumble. Derek Randall, who was dropped twice by Lever, scored 49 off forty-nine balls before French and Hemmings fiddled and lunged their way to the game's final delivery which Hemmings despatched for the winning runs.

Essex's last appearance in the Benson and Hedges final was against Leicestershire in 1998. After losing Stuart Law, Paul Prichard (92) and Nasser Hussain (88) put on 134 for the second wicket as Essex reached 268 for seven in their allotted fifty overs. Devastating bowling by Mark Ilott and Ashley Cowan reduced Leicestershire to 31 for six and though Paul Nixon hit one or two lusty blows, they were all out for 76 in 27.4 overs, leaving Essex the winners by 192 runs.

Essex's Benson and Hedges records include:

Highest innings total: 388 for seven v Scotland at Chelmsford in 1992.
Lowest innings total: 61 v Lancashire at Chelmsford in 1992.
Highest individual innings: 198* by Graham Gooch v Sussex at Hove in 1982.
Best Bowling Performance: John Lever 5 for 13 v Middlesex at Lord's in 1985.
Highest partnership: 268* by Graham Gooch and Keith Fletcher for the
third wicket v Sussex at Hove in 1982.
Most Gold Awards: Twenty-two by Graham Gooch.

BEST XI

Selecting a best team can be a fascinating relaxation but it can also be highly provocative. For players were at their best in different decades and comparisons can be odious and the more one thinks of all the players who have represented Essex, the more difficult the task of selecting the best eleven becomes.

Although it was not easy to leave out players of the calibre of Stan Nichols, Peter Smith and Nasser Hussain, below is my best Essex team:

1 Graham Gooch
2 Percy Perrin
3 Jack O'Connor
4 Keith Fletcher (Captain)
5 Charles McGahey
6 Trevor Bailey
7 Johnny Douglas
8 Brian Taylor
9 Charles Kortright
10 John Lever
11 Walter Mead

BOYCE, KEITH

As a youngster in the Caribbean, Keith Boyce's life was built around school and sport and his love for both cricket and football brought him many a cuff around his ears for being late home. After leaving junior school, he attended Coleridge Parry Secondary School and it was here that he wore pads and batting gloves for the first time. He also captained the school side, bowling quickly to open and then reverting to leg breaks if the wicket was turning a little. Batting came naturally to Keith Boyce and by the age of twenty, he was representing Barbados in inter-island cricket.

He had been seen by Trevor Bailey during the Rothman Cavaliers tour of the West Indies in 1964-65 and had been included in the Bajaan team in their second match against the touring Cavaliers. He impressed Bailey with his all-round performance – his hitting power, fast bowling and tremendous fielding. The result was that he followed the tourists to England to start qualifying for Essex.

The young all-rounder from Barbados had a wonderful debut during his qualifying period, taking 13 wickets for 108 runs against Cambridge University including first innings figures of nine for 61.

He made his first appearance in the County Championship in 1967 and came close to achieving the double in that first season, scoring more than 900 runs and capturing 81 wickets.

He hit his maiden century against Hampshire at Valentine's Park in June 1969. His unbeaten 147 was made in three hours and contained 21 fours. He also hit 50 in twenty-three minutes against Lancashire in a John Player League match and his all-round ability won him a single-wicket tournament at Lord's.

Boyce was an Essex man through and through in spite of playing on a regular basis for Barbados and later in his career representing the West Indies. The Essex crowds thrilled to Boyce's exploits for his great determination to win every game was apparent for all to see. He was a most exciting and unpredictable player. He was a great one-day cricketer, possessing the ability to change the course of a match within a couple of overs, with either bat or ball.

In the 1971 John Player League he performed the hat-trick against

Keith Boyce.

Somerset and destroyed Lancashire on a wet day at Old Trafford with figures of eight for 26.

Boyce appeared in twenty-one Tests for the West Indies and when they beat England by 158 runs at the Oval in 1973, he hit 72, batting at Number Nine, and then followed it with five for 70 and six for 77.

The following summer he performed the hat-trick again as Essex beat Warwickshire in the county championship and was selected as one of *Wisden's* Five Cricketers of the Year

During the 1976 season, Boyce was forced to miss a number of matches with a knee injury. It came as a great loss when, after a serious knee operation, he was forced to retire. Boyce, who had scored 6,848 runs and taken 662 wickets, was a dedicated Essex cricketer. When he was given the news that he would not be able to play again, he asked the Essex committee to keep his registration just in case he got better. Sadly this most popular of Essex players died in 1996.

BRENTWOOD

Of the many grounds used by Essex, probably the most attractive was the tree-surrounded acres of Brentwood.

The earliest county game there was in 1922 but Essex did not return again until 1934 when there was sensational scoring in the six days' play. Kent were the visitors in the glorious days of Frank Woolley, 'Tich' Freeman and Leslie Ames and they opened with Ashdown and Fagg on a perfect wicket. Ashdown made a chanceless 332, Frank Woolley dropped at two, amassed 172 and put on 352 with Ashdown in a little over three hours. Ames followed, had an escape at 30 and went on to 202 not out and Kent declared at 803 for four. Essex replied with 408 but spin was beginning to bite and Freeman and Wright bowled them out for 203 in the follow-on. In the next three days, Essex defeated Surrey by an innings and 192 runs in another high-scoring game and in the six days' play 2,362 runs were scored and eight individual centuries compiled.

BRIGHTER CRICKET

In 1952, a Brighter Cricket Table was compiled by the *News Chronicle*, based on runs per hundred balls received. Essex headed this table with 50.44 runs against 49.96 by the county champions, Surrey, and won the newspaper's award of a silver salver in the year of its inception. The county won the trophy again the following year, for in spite of the wet wickets, they continued to play attractive cricket under the leadership of Doug Insole.

BROTHERS

There have been a number of instances of brothers playing for Essex including Johnny and Cecil Douglas and George and Lawrie Eastman but perhaps the most famous brothers to play for the county were Hubert and Claude Ashton.

Both men were fine cricketers but sadly neither played as much county cricket as Essex would have liked. Both of them captained Cambridge University, as did a third brother Gilbert, who played for Worcestershire.

BUCKENHAM, CLAUDE

During the early part of his Essex career, Claude Buckenham was rated as one of the deadliest pace bowlers in the country. He was a tall man, though rather sparingly built. He bowled with great speed and a good, high delivery and would have made a greater name for himself if he had been given stronger support in the field.

Buckenham's best figures for the county, eight for 33, came against Sussex at Leyton in 1904. The following year, Essex beat the Australians by 19 runs, the only county side to do so. Buckenham and Tremlin took all twenty wickets between them with Buckenham having figures of 12 for 137. In 1906, Buckenham topped the one hundred wicket mark and finished the season with 135 wickets at an average of 24.13 runs each.

His performances with the ball led to him winning selection for Leveson-Gower's team to tour South Africa in 1909-10. He played in the first four Tests, taking twenty-one wickets at an average of 28.23, his best performance being five for 115 at Johannesburg.

Buckenham's ability to hit a cricket ball hard brought him two first-class hundreds and he often played a useful innings when runs were required. At the end of the 1912 season, he decided to accept a position in Scotland. He was assisting Forfar but returned to Essex to play in the last five games of 1914. After the First World War he became coach at Repton School.

If those missed chances had not been missed, I wonder just how many wickets Claude Buckenham would have taken – as it was, he captured 934 wickets at a cost of 26.36 runs apiece.

BULL, FREDERICK

Frederick Bull was an off-break bowler of great promise and although his career was to be all too short, his promise was realised in the four years following his Essex debut in 1895.

In 1896, Bull headed the county's bowling averages, taking seventy-four wickets, but he would have wanted to forget his first game in the championship. He dropped the great Surrey batsman Bobby Abel off Kortright's bowling when he had only made two – and Abel went on to score 231. Also that summer, he was one of five Essex players involved in the Gentlemen v Players match at the Oval. He was without doubt the hero of the match, taking eight for 94 in the Players' first innings. At this time, Bull was only twenty and had been selected for this representative match purely on merit.

In 1897, Bull produced the best figures of his career, nine for 93 against Surrey. He was so highly rated by Pelham Warner that he was chosen to tour America in the close season and had a very successful trip, taking 43 wickets at only 13.86 runs apiece, the greatest number taken by any member of the side.

There had been queries over Bull's bowling action. The legality of quite a few players' action had been questioned and certainly not everyone thought Bull's action fair.

In 1898 he captured 101 wickets at 21.40 runs each and was chosen as one of *Wisden's* Five Cricketers of the Year. After two seasons of topping the hundred wicket mark, Bull took only 65 in 1899 and the following year gave way to Bill Reeves, Bull's form having been so indifferent.

He moved up north and after a season playing for East Lancashire, spent two years as professional with Perth. He then returned to Lancashire to play for Rishton.

He was often a moody man but it was a shock when on 16 September 1910 he was found drowned at St Annes near Blackpool, his coat and trouser pockets being filled with stones. It was a sad end for one who had served Essex so well, though only for a short period.

C

CAMBRIDGE UNIVERSITY

In 1910, in Essex's first first-class meeting with Cambridge University at Fenner's, the Light Blues were beaten by an innings as Perrin and Gillingham, who both scored centuries, added 291 for the third wicket.

When the two sides met in 1949, Cambridge University scored 441 for one declared with John Dewes (204 not out) and Hubert Doggart (219 not out) sharing a second wicket partnership of 429 – an English record.

Keith Boyce made his Essex debut against Cambridge University in 1966, taking nine for 61 and four for 47 as his pace proved too much for the Light Blues' batsmen.

Graham Gooch always enjoyed playing against Cambridge University and in 1980 hit 205, the first double-hundred of his career. In 1983 he once again took the Cambridge bowlers apart, hitting 174 in an opening stand of 263 with Brian Hardie.

CAPTAINS

This is the complete list of Essex's captains.

1876-1882	James Round	1939(contd)	Frederick St George
1883-1888	Charles Green		Unwin and Denys Wilcox
1889-1891	Cyril Buxton	1946-1949	Tom Pearce
1892-1894	Alfred Lucas	1950	Tom Pearce and Doug
1895-1902	Hugh Owen		Insole
1903	Charles Kortright	1951-1960	Doug Insole
1904-1906	Frederick Fane	1961-1966	Trevor Bailey
1907-1910	Charles McGahey	1967-1973	Brian Taylor
1911-1928	Johnny Douglas (Percy	1974-1985	Keith Fletcher
	Perrin deputised in his	1986-1987	Graham Gooch
	absence in 1926)	1988	Keith Fletcher
1929-1932	Harold Morris	1989-1994	Graham Gooch
1933-1938	Tom Pearce and Denys	1995-1998	Paul Prichard
	Wilcox	1999	Nasser Hussain
1939	John Stephenson	2000	Ronnie Irani

CARLING SINGLE WICKET

Essex and England all-rounder Barry Knight won the 1964 Carling Single Wicket competition at Lord's beating Northamptonshire's Colin Milburn in the final.

CARPENTER, HERBERT

The son of Robert Carpenter, one of the greatest batsmen of the United All-England and Cambridgeshire sides of the mid-nineteenth century, he made his Essex debut before the county had been granted first-class status in 1885 but made little impression.

He was instrumental in helping the county to the higher grade and in 1894 he opened the batting in Essex's first match as a first-class county against Leicestershire.

In 1895 he became the first Essex batsman to score more than 1,000 runs in a season, hitting a run a minute 153 against Somerset at Taunton before being run out. Over the next few seasons, Carpenter proved himself to be a batsman of the highest quality and in 1900, hit 1,468 runs including four centuries. He exceeded 1,000 runs again in 1901, scoring centuries in both innings, 127 and 104 against Kent at Leyton – the second Essex batsman (after McGahey) to score two separate hundreds in a first-class match. He had been in dispute with the committee in 1902 and did not play at all the following summer but returned in 1904 to hit the highest score of his career, 199 against Surrey at the Oval.

In 1911, along with John Freeman, he had the unusual distinction of sharing in century partnerships in each innings of the match against Surrey at Leyton. In 1914 he hit the last of his twenty-five centuries in first-class cricket – an unbeaten 126 against Worcestershire, sharing in an unfinished stand of 237 with 'Jack' Russell.

After the First World War, he returned to play in the last few matches of the 1920 season. He was now in his fifty-second year and had given great service to the county.

Herbert Carpenter was without doubt one of the greatest professional batsmen never to play for England. He was a superb player for Essex, not just in terms of runs scored – 13,043 – but because of all the advice and coaching he gave to others.

CATCHES

The most catches in an innings by an Essex player is five, a feat achieved by six county players. Frank Vigar performed the feat on three occasions – v Middlesex at Westcliff 1946, v Northamptonshire at Brentwood 1946 and v Surrey at the Oval in 1951. Frank Gillingham's five catches were v Surrey at the Oval in 1919, Stan Nichols' v Sussex at Hove in 1926, Doug Insole's v Lancashire at Blackpool in 1958, Graham Gooch's v Gloucestershire at Cheltenham in 1982 and Nick Knight's v Warwickshire at Edgbaston in 1994.

Former Essex and England captain Keith Fletcher holds the county record for the most catches in a season with forty two in 1966 and for the most catches in a career, a total of 519 – 133 more than second-placed Graham Gooch.

CENTURIES

The first century scored by an Essex player came from the bat of Hugh Owen with 109 against Oxford University at Leyton in 1894. The first, and his only championship hundred, was scored by James Burns who made 114 against Warwickshire at Edgbaston in the Essex's first championship match in May 1895. The highest score for the county and only triple century is Percy Perrin's 343 not out against Derbyshire in 1904, yet despite his mammoth innings, Essex lost by nine wickets.

Of the 109 individual batsmen who have scored centuries for Essex only five – Jack O'Connor, Doug Insole, Ken McEwan, Jack Russell and Graham Gooch – had scored their hundreds all against County Championship opponents. However, Gooch has gone one better than the others, having also scored a century against recent County Championship newcomers, Durham.

The following players have scored the most centuries for Essex:

1	Graham Gooch	94	7	Keith Fletcher	45
2	Jack O'Connor	71	8	Paul Prichard	31
3	Percy Perrin	65	9	Gordon Barker	30
4	Jack Russell	62	10=	Nasser Hussain	29
5	Ken McEwan	52		Charles McGahey	29
6	Doug Insole	48			

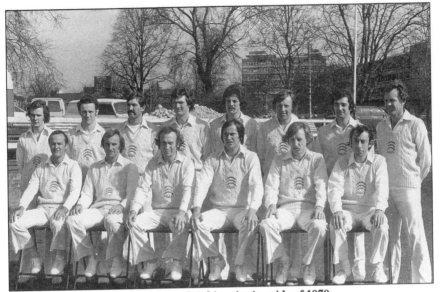
Essex's championship-winning side of 1979

CHAMPIONSHIPS

Essex have won the County Championship on six occasions. Their first success came in 1979 when they got off to a flying start and never looked back. The county had been on the brink of winning something for years but always seemed to fail at the crucial time. Having finished second in 1978, they were ready for an assault on the top.

There were some who said that their flying start was due to extraordinary good luck with the foul weather which considerably disrupted the progress of their challengers. Essex's performances were impressive and if they did have a bit of luck with the weather, then it was no more than they deserved. For John Lever, Essex's 'Man of the Season', there was only one minor disappointment, for he took 99 championship wickets instead of the coveted hundred. Essex were certainly a team of all-rounders – McEwan hit 208 not out against Warwickshire at Edgbaston, six players hit centuries, and wicketkeeper Neil Smith scored an unbeaten 90. But John Lever's purple patch carried Essex to the title, improving his career best innings figures once and match figures twice.

Essex became County Champions for a second time in 1983 when they nosed out Middlesex into second place. They owed a great deal to the superlative batting of Ken McEwan, the only player to top 2,000 runs in championship cricket at an average of 68.36. However, it was not simple batting that carried Essex through as John Lever took 97 wickets at an average of 16.80 and Norbert Phillip 68 at 19.67. David East behind the stumps had an outstanding season with sixty-five victims and won the Gordon's Gin Wicketkeeper of the Year award. Sixteen centuries were scored by Essex players in the championship, half of them by McEwan.

Essex retained their county title in 1984 but that fact conceals the high drama during the final stages of the summer months. It was to be either Essex or Nottinghamshire but the ultimate winner was not decided until the final over. Nottinghamshire were playing Somerset at Taunton and needed 14 runs from the last over to produce enough points to overtake Essex. Their last pair were at the wicket but after Mike Bore had hit ten runs off the first three deliveries and blocked the fourth, he was caught off the fifth. It was a splendid season for Essex, a fine side admirably led by Keith Fletcher. England's tragic loss of Graham Gooch was certainly a great gain for Essex and with Pringle and Foster not called upon and the superb bowling of John Lever, Essex had the most balanced of sides.

In 1986, Essex won their third championship in four years with something to spare. Shrugging off injuries and Test calls, they battled through a mockery of a summer to finish 28 points ahead of Gloucestershire who had made most of the early running. John Childs, formerly of Gloucestershire, took 89 wickets at 16.28 apiece and in a seven-match spell took 48 wickets at 12.37 runs including 16 in two successive innings at Colchester.

Although Warwickshire led the County Championship table for most of the 1991 season, Essex overcame a 51 point deficit to end the longest first-class season as County Champions. Their fifth title in thirteen years ended a sequence of three near misses and was a tribute to the club's policy of ruthless efficiency. Having dismissed reigning champions Middlesex for just 51, Essex ended the first day on 385 for three with Graham Gooch having completed his ninth double hundred in first-class cricket.

Nasser Hussain enjoyed his most prolific summer and shared in two triple century partnerships. Neil Foster contributed greatly to Essex's success, taking 91 wickets at 21.97 and leading the side in Gooch's absence.

Essex retained the title in 1992. It was finally achieved by the emphatic margin of 41 points after a dismal start to the season. Guided by Keith Fletcher for the last time before he assumed the mantle of England team manager, Essex had stormed to a 51 point lead by the middle of July, to threaten the earliest date by which the championship had been decided. However, with Mark Waugh's departure for Australia's Sri Lanka mission and an injury to Neil Foster, a one-horse race was averted.

CHELMSFORD

The county ground at New Writtle Street, Chelmsford has been the head-quarters of Essex County Cricket Club since 1967 and the majority of their matches are staged there. Essex first played a County Championship match here in 1926 when their opponents were Somerset. At that time most matches were still played at Leyton.

Since the installation of a drainage system in 1982, Chelmsford is one of the best-drained grounds on the county circuit. Previously, the ground was liable to flood because of the close proximity of the River Can and the high water table. For some time the cricket field was used as an emergency helicopter pad for the nearby hospital, until the casualty department was moved to other premises in the town.

Many memorable performances have taken place here, including Wally Hammond's 244 in 1928 and Sir Learie Constantine's bowling for the West Indies in 1939 when he took 13 for 91. In 1977 Ken McEwan hit a magnificent 218 against Sussex and six years later, Surrey were bowled out for just 14.

The ground hosted international cricket in 1983 when a World Cup match was staged between Australia and India and again in 1999 when Bangladesh played New Zealand and Zimbabwe met South Africa.

CHILDS, JOHN

John Childs began his first-class career with Gloucestershire after being spotted playing Minor Counties cricket for Devon. After ten mixed years in his native West Country, Childs was left pondering on an uncertain future with Gloucestershire at the relatively young age (for a spinner) of thirty-three. Childs then wrote to most other first-class counties and was delighted by an approach from Keith Fletcher who was seeking to strengthen his Essex side after the retirement of Ray East. Childs jumped at the chance of joining the County Champions and despite a disappointing return of just five wickets in 1985, due in the main to injury and poor weather, he was retained for the following season.

Essex's first match in 1986 was on a slow, damp turner at Northampton and in one innings, Childs took as many wickets as he had managed during the whole of the previous season. He went on to take a

career best 89 wickets, including eight for 58 against Gloucestershire, his former county, playing an important role in the Essex team which won the championship again. Not surprisingly he was named as one of the *Wisden's* Five Cricketers of the Year.

Two years later, Childs was stepping up even further to the Test arena, winning two caps against the mighty West Indies. He bowled well enough to be selected for the winter tour of India but it was cancelled because of the South African 'connections' of several members of the team.

Forming an excellent alliance with Peter Such, Childs regularly took fifty wickets in a season, playing the last of 187 games for Essex in which he captured 530 first-class wickets at 27.77 runs apiece in 1996.

John Childs.

COLCHESTER

Essex first played a County Championship match at Castle Park in June 1914 when they beat Warwickshire by 193 runs. Essex tried a Colchester week in 1920 and the first match was a triumph for Philip Mead whose 178 not out for Hampshire helped them to victory by an innings and 62 runs. Gloucestershire then rubbed salt into the wounds by winning the next match by an innings and 56 runs. After a break of some years, Essex returned to Colchester in 1934 and have played there continuously since.

Colchester is the only ground on which a player has scored a double century in each innings of a match as Arthur Fagg did for Kent in 1938. Colchester is also a happy hunting ground for former skipper Doug Insole who scored his only double-century in first-class cricket, 219 not out against Yorkshire in 1949. The ground was totally submerged in water in 1958 with chairs and forms floating across the ground and the Essex v Leicestershire game was abandoned. The match against Nottinghamshire, due to start the next day, was transferred to the Garrison Ground at the top of the hill, rather than at the foot as Castle Park is. Gordon Barker and Arthur Fagg both made hundreds before lunch and Peter Smith achieved the best bowling performance of his life when he took nine for 77 against Middlesex in 1947. In 1982 in the Sunday League match against Warwickshire an aggregate of 600 runs was amassed.

CUTMORE, JIM

In his early days, Jim Cutmore had intended qualifying for Glamorgan – he would probably have been at home in the Welsh valleys with his fine tenor singing voice – but Essex had heard of his success in club cricket and signed him on.

In 1925, after making 95 against Derbyshire, he was awarded his county cap and celebrated by making an unbeaten 134 against Lancashire as he went on to pass 1,000 runs for the season – a feat he achieved in each of the next eleven seasons. Cutmore's highest score for the county, 238 not out came against Gloucestershire in 1927.

In 1930 Lancashire had to beat Essex in the final game of the season at Blackpool to win the County Championship. Needing 286 to win, Essex were bowled out for 111 but Cutmore showed his fighting qualities with a superb 77 on a bad wicket. No other Essex player made double figures. The Essex side toasted the red rose county as champions in Champagne provided by the Lancashire president – Jim Cutmore rendering one of his songs.

In 1935, Cutmore was instrumental in Essex beating the touring South Africans by seven wickets, hitting 72 and 59 not out. The visiting Indians also suffered at the hands of Jim Cutmore the following season at Brentwood. Cutmore scored 137 as he and Peter Smith (105) put on 214 for the eighth wicket. After his superb century against the Indians, his form began to desert him and he was not re-engaged for the 1937 season.

When on form, Cutmore, who scored 15,937 runs for the county, was a most entertaining batsman. He was a bit of an enigma. He had plenty of confidence but it was often misplaced and his temperament was not altogether suited to the hurly-burly of first-class cricket.

D

DEATHS

A number of Essex cricketers have lost their life in unusual circumstances. Henry Pickett, who took all ten wickets for 32 runs against Leicestershire in 1895, disappeared from his home on 27 September 1907 and his body was found on the beach at Aberavon six days later. However, it was not until the turn of the year that his fate was known, for only then were some articles found on the body identified as his.

Frederick Bull met with a similar tragic death. After resigning as the county's secretary he took up a business appointment in Blackburn before playing as a professional for both East Lancashire and Rishton in the Lancashire League. On 16 September 1910 he was found drowned at St Annes-on-Sea. A handkerchief was tied round his neck in which was knotted a heavy stone and his coat and trouser pockets were also filled with stones.

Essex and England captain, Johnny Douglas, drowned on 19 December 1930 when he was returning home from a business trip on the Finnish ship *Oberon*. The *Oberon* collided with its sister ship, *Arcturus,* in the dense fog off the coast of Denmark and Douglas lost his life while trying, unsuccessfully, to save his father.

Charles McGahey died in January 1935 after slipping on a greasy pavement on Christmas Day and damaging a finger. Septic poisoning set in and proved fatal.

Victims of the Second World War were Ken Farnes, who had been sent to Canada for training, returned to these shores to become a night-fighter pilot. He was killed on 20 October 1941 when the plane he was piloting crashed. All-rounder Lawrie Eastman died in hospital on 17 April 1941 after being injured in an air raid when serving as an ARP warden.

In 1942 Claude Ashton, who also played international football for England, lost his life in a flying disaster.

DEFEATS

Essex's heaviest defeat came in 1948 when the touring Australians beat the side by an innings and 451 runs at Southend. The county's biggest defeat in the championship was in 1932 when Yorkshire won by an innings and 313 runs in the match played at Leyton. During this match, Percy Holmes and Herbert Sutcliffe of Yorkshire created a new world record by adding 555 for the first wicket.

DERBYSHIRE

Founded in 1870, Derbyshire's solitary championship title came in 1936. The county also won the inaugural Nat West Trophy tournament in 1981, the Sunday League in 1990 and the Benson and Hedges Cup in 1993.

When Essex met Derbyshire at Leyton in 1901, Bill Reeves took the last five Derbyshire wickets in eleven balls without conceding a run.

In the match at Chesterfield in 1904, Percy Perrin scored 343 not out. He hit 68 fours although it was alleged some years later that fourteen of his boundaries would now have been classed as sixes. Perrin's innings remains the only triple century ever made by an Essex player in county cricket and as unbelievable as it may seem, Essex lost.

The 1921 match played at Leyton was a personal triumph for the Essex and England captain, Johnny Douglas, who took nine for 47 as Derbyshire were bowled out for 114. In reply, Essex were struggling at 37 for five but eventually ended the first day at 138 for seven. Douglas was still there, and after Derbyshire grabbed an early wicket on the second day, he was joined by Hare. He and Douglas added 251 for the ninth wicket before he was caught at mid-off for 98. Douglas, who had scored 210 not out, had recorded his best figures with both bat and ball.

Another Essex batting record was established in the 1947 meeting at Chesterfield. After feeling unwell, Peter Smith came in at Number.11 to join Frank Vigar. They proceeded to put on 218 for the last wicket after Essex had been 199 for nine. Peter Smith scored 163, the highest score ever made by a Number.11 batsman. Not surprisingly he was chosen as one of *Wisden's* Five Cricketers of the Year.

The following summer, his cousin Ray Smith scored his maiden century,

112 in the match at Colchester in 63 minutes. It was the fastest hundred of the season.

When Jim Laker made his Essex debut in the match against Derbyshire, Gordon Barker had the dubious distinction of dropping a chance off the England spin bowler's first ball.

DODDS, DICKIE

Dickie Dodds had played for Middlesex 2nd XI before the Second World War and in various army teams in the Aldershot area and in India where he made his first-class debut.

In 1946, his first season with Essex, Dodds played as an amateur, scoring 1,050 runs including two hundreds. One of these came in the record-breaking partnership of 270 for the first wicket against Surrey at the Oval. His partner was Sonny Avery, who scored 210. Dodds scored 103.

Dodds was such a hard-hitting opening batsman that he enjoyed nothing more than facing a fast bowler and quite often would hit the opening ball he faced for six. In 1947 he turned professional and hit 2,147 runs, yet scored only one century – a tribute to his consistency. This season he was selected for the MCC against the South African tourists, scoring 80 and 25. Rather surprisingly it was his last representative match for he was never considered for a Gentlemen v Players fixture or international honours.

Dodds continued to impress, regularly scoring well over 1,000 runs a season at a rate of more than 40 runs per hour. He was regarded as the fastest scoring opener in the county and continued to hit the first balls of a number of innings for six and in 1953 hit the first delivery from Sussex's Ian Thomson onto the pavilion roof. No respecter of people, Dodds hit both Lindwall and Miller all over the ground for a quick-fire 58 out of the first 70 runs scored in the match against the Australians.

In November 1957 Dodds announced that he was going to devote the whole of his benefit fund, which amounted to £2,325, to Moral Rearmament, for which he was a tireless worker.

One of the greatest cricket entertainers of the era, he scored 18,565 runs for Essex and scored 1,000 runs a season on thirteen consecutive occasions from his debut.

DOUBLE

The feat of scoring 1,000 runs and taking 100 wickets in a season has been performed twenty times by six Essex players:

	Year	Runs	Average	Wickets	Average
Stan Nichols	1929	1281	29.11	100	25.56
	1932	1381	32.11	106	25.52
	1933	1311	29.13	120	21.55
	1935	1171	24.39	138	15.70
	1936	1224	29.85	108	18.47
	1937	1159	25.19	136	18.56
	1938	1310	35.40	160	18.31
	1939	1363	35.86	119	17.84
Johnny Douglas	1914	1151	39.68	118	18.88
	1920	1200	35.29	124	20.98
	1921	1211	46.57	110	18.10
	1923	1043	30.67	139	22.01
Trevor Bailey	1960	1597	40.94	113	20.26
	1961	1179	29.47	120	20.25
	1962	1420	36.41	111	21.00
Ray Smith	1947	1201	27.93	118	36.74
	1950	1109	23.59	101	34.57
Barry Knight	1963	1412	30.04	125	21.94
	1965	1001	21.76	121	18.52
Peter Smith	1947	1065	23.66	172	27.13

DOUGLAS, JOHNNY

John William Henry Tyler Douglas made his debut for Essex against Yorkshire in 1901, being bowled by Hirst for nought in both innings – not the best of debuts for a player who was destined to become a great force in Essex cricket. Yorkshire were again the opponents in 1905 when Douglas made his first great impact on the game. He took five Yorkshire wickets in eight balls including the first hat-trick by an Essex player in first-class cricket.

In August 1908 he had his greatest triumph to date when he scored his maiden century in first-class cricket, 102 against Sussex.

His long graduation in consolidating his county place was partly due to his talents as a middle-weight boxer, which brought him the 1905 Amateur Championship and the 1908 Olympic title; and as a footballer who gained an England amateur cap against Bohemia..

In 1909, playing for an England XI against Australia, he scored 102, helping A E Knight of Leicestershire to put on 284 for the first wicket.

Despite his limited experience he became Essex captain in 1911, demanding better fielding and a better team spirit. Leading by example, he scored a brilliant 176 against Nottinghamshire at Trent Bridge and was chosen to represent the Gentlemen against the Players at both the Oval and Lord's. It was on the strength of his performances in these matches that he was chosen to go to Australia.

'Plum' Warner was captain, but after playing in the opening match at Adelaide he was taken ill and did not play again. Douglas was appointed captain and after losing the first Test he led England to four successive victories.

As a captain, Douglas was loyal to those under him and they gave him their loyalty and many of them their love in return. He was no great tactician as a captain, for he relied entirely on endeavour and inspiration. He often encouraged aspiring young bowlers by placing a half-crown on top of the stumps when he was batting in the nets. The first one to dismiss him gained the reward.

In 1913-14 he was chosen to lead the MCC side to tour South Africa. England won the five-match series by four Tests to nil, Douglas hitting his one and only Test century, 119 at Durban.

He returned to England for the 1914 season very much a hero. In the game against Surrey, he bowled the great Jack Hobbs twice. Hobbs always considered him one of the best bowlers he ever faced. Douglas ended the summer with 1,151 runs and 118 wickets – becoming the first Essex player to do the double – and not surprisingly he was named as one of *Wisden's* Five Cricketers of the Year.

In 1921, Douglas turned in some remarkable performances with both bat and ball. He had an outstanding match against Derbyshire, turning in his career best with an innings of 210 not out and taking nine for 47. The Essex side finished third bottom of the County Championship table that season, only winning five of its matches, yet Douglas's performances in those games was outstanding as the following figures show:

Innings	Not Out	Highest score	Runs	Average
7	3	210*	562	140.50
Overs	Maidens	Runs	Wickets	Average
202.3	48	516	53	9.76

In 1923, Douglas hit 147 not out against Gloucestershire as he and Jack O'Connor put on 206 for the sixth wicket. Their stand has been equalled but never beaten as a county record. His 146 wickets that summer included a hat-trick against Sussex at Leyton.

Over the next few seasons, Douglas struggled to produce anything like his best form and at the end of the 1928 season, after which he had scored 17,915 runs and taken 1,443 wickets, he left the county. The club had suggested that he should resign as captain but Douglas refused and fought the committee in what was a protracted and sad business. He was invited to become a member of the selection committee and to play as often as possible for Essex but he did neither.

In 1930 Douglas was drowned when returning home from a business trip (see page 29). Johnny Douglas had given his life to Essex cricket. He had captained the county for eighteen years – only W G Grace led a county for a longer period – and his own performances had brought great honour to the club.

DURHAM

Founded in 1882, Durham entered the County Championship in 1992. Highlights in the meetings between the two counties have been few and far between but in the 1995 match at Chelmsford, Durham's Alan Walker produced what are the northern county's best match figures. After taking eight for 118 in Essex's first innings, he took six for 59 to finish with match figures of 14 for 177.

E

EAST, RAY

It was Peter Smith who persuaded the East family that Ray, at the age of sixteen, possessed a talent that made professional cricket a suitable career for him to pursue. His early preparation for the first-class game mostly involved playing for the Suffolk village of Brantham.

It was in 1968 that East produced his best overall bowling figures when he took 15 for 115 in the match against Warwickshire at Leyton. Ray East turned the ball a great deal and once performed the hat-trick in a Test trial. His feat however was unrewarded and he never won a place in the England side. He did in the 1973-74 close season tour South Africa with the D H Robbins XI.

Ray East.

His batting had been improving steadily over the seasons and in 1976 he made his one and only first-class century, scoring 113 in the match against Hampshire at Chelmsford. The following summer he produced the best figures of his career, taking eight for 30 against Nottinghamshire at Ilford as Essex won by six wickets. His best season was 1978 when he took 92 wickets – it was also his benefit year.

Ray East's humorous exploits are legendary. There was the time he was brought on at the end of the day by Keith Fletcher after the seamers had bowled all morning and afternoon. His reaction was to cup his hands and yell out 'East' towards the scorers as if they had called for the bowler's name as they often do in club cricket when an unknown bowler appears. On one occasion when several Essex players went down with a flu virus, he walked up and down in front of the dressing room with a placard marked 'UNCLEAN'. Legendary they may be but they hid the fact that he was one of only nine Essex bowlers to have taken more than 1,000 wickets for the county. ·

EASTMAN, LAWRIE

Originally an amateur player, Lawrie Eastman's ambition to take up medicine as a profession had been thwarted by the First World War, in which he won the Distinguished Conduct Medal and Military Medal. His love for the game of cricket had been noticed by Johnny Douglas and Percy Perrin and he was invited to play for the county in their match against Gloucestershire at Bristol.Although the game was marred by rain, Eastman's medium-pace bowling brought him figures of five for 53 including a spell of three wickets in four balls. In the following game at Lord's, he went in at Number 10 and hit a superb 91 as he and Russell added what was then a ninth wicket record stand of 184.

In 1922, Eastman produced his best bowling figures for the county, taking seven for 28 against Somerset at Taunton and two years later, after being appointed assistant-secretary at Leyton, hit his maiden first-class century against Surrey. He was by now developing into a hard-hitting opening batsman, making his highest score of 161 against Derbyshire in 1929.

In his early days, Eastman bowled medium-pace but served Essex best when he changed to spin. He could turn the ball both ways but was particularly deadly with the leg-break. Against Somerset at Weston-super-Mare in 1934, he took four for nought in the space of a couple of overs.

Eastman once commented that he batted in every position except Number 11. In his benefit match against Middlesex at Southend, he was forced to bat last as he was suffering from water on the knee. Essex unfortunately lost by five runs but if Eastman had not injured his knee, they would most surely have won. He did not enjoy the best of health but still managed to score 12,965 runs and capture 975 wickets. When war broke out, he helped the London counties and was proud of being captain when the side first appeared at Lord's. During the hostilities, Eastman worked as an ARP warden and when he was on duty he was injured by a high-explosive bomb and severely shocked. He died after undergoing an operation at Harefield Sanatorium in April 1941, aged just forty-three.

EDMEADES, BRIAN

Brian Edmeades had played for both London and Essex Schoolboys in representative cricket, scoring runs and picking up wickets as a change bowler, a performance noted by Essex coach Frank Rist. On leaving school, he was offered a trial and soon on the county staff.

He scored his maiden first-class century, 135 against Lancashire at Old Trafford in 1946, before being bowled by Brian Statham. It was his most successful season so far. He was awarded his county cap the following summer when, for the only time in his career, he took ten wickets in a match, including seven for 43 as Essex beat Derbyshire by 85 runs.

Edmeades was a great favourite with the Essex crowds. In 1966, he topped the county's bowling averages with 106 wickets at 18.59 runs apiece, producing the best figures of his career, seven for 37 against Glamorgan at Leyton. As the years went by, he began to establish himself as one of the most consistent opening batsmen on the county circuit and in 1970 he scored 1,620 runs at an average of 35.21.

Edmeades missed most of the 1971 season with an eye injury but returned with a vengeance the following summer and hit the highest score of his career, 163 against Leicestershire at Leyton. His career ended with him as an attacking opening batsman but his medium-pace bowling ensured that he played a vital part in any match, especially the one-day game. In 1973 he took five for 22 against Leicestershire at Ilford in the Benson and Hedges Cup and in 1976 he hit 125 not out against Minor Counties(East) at Norwich in sharing a second wicket stand of 172 with Ken McEwan.

Retiring at the end of the 1976 season after scoring 12,593 runs and capturing 374 wickets, he continued to play professionally for five years with Clydesdale with whom he won cups and league titles that had eluded him with Essex.

Brian Edmeades was an all-rounder whose exciting approach to the game typified the county which specialised in all-rounders.

ENGLAND TEST CRICKETERS

Essex's most capped England player is Graham Gooch who won 118 caps. The full list is:

Trevor Bailey	61	Doug Insole	9
Claude Buckenham	4	Ronnie Irani	3
John Childs	2	Barry Knight	29
Johnny Douglas	23	John Lever	21
Freddie Fane	14	Charlie McGahey	2
Ken Farnes	15	Walter Mead	1
Keith Fletcher	59	Stan Nichols	14
Neil Foster	25	Jack O'Connor	4
Paul Gibbs	8	Derek Pringle	19
Graham Gooch	118	Jack Russell	10
Robin Hobbs	7	Peter Smith	4
Nasser Hussain	54	Peter Such	11
Mark Ilott	5	Sailor Young	2

F

FANE, FREDERICK

Frederick Luther Fane was born at Curragh Camp in Ireland where his father, who played for both Ireland and Essex in pre first-class days, was serving with his regiment. He spent three years in the Charterhouse XI before moving on to Oxford where he played in two Varsity matches.

In 1899, Fane became the first Essex batsman to make a double century when he scored 207 against Leicestershire at Grace Road. He succeeded Charles Kortright as Essex captain in 1904, coming to the post at a very difficult time. The county club had narrowly avoided liquidation and the nucleus of their bowling attack would not be playing. Fane was unusual in that although he captained both Essex and England, he was a reluctant captain who undertook the task with considerable reservations.

In 1902-03 he toured Australia and New Zealand as a member of Lord Hawke's side, scoring more than 500 runs with a brilliant hundred against New Zealand at Christchurch. In 1905-06 he went to South Africa under Warner and headed the batting averages with 607 runs at 37.93. He hit fifties in the second and fourth Test matches and a magnificent 143 in the third Test at Johannesburg.

In 1906, his last year as captain of Essex, Fane had his best season, scoring 1,572 runs at 34.93, and leading the county to seventh place in the championship. In 1907-08 he was a member of the MCC side which toured Australia. He scored 133 in the first match at Perth and when Jones was taken ill, it was Fane who took over the captaincy for the first two Tests, thus becoming the first Essex cricketer to captain his country.

Fane, who had resigned as captain of Essex because he was unable to commit himself to playing on a regular basis, continued to score freely. In 1911 he hit 217 against Surrey at the Oval. It was the highest score of his career and was made in front of the future kings, Edward VIII and George VI.

After the First World War, during which he was awarded the Military Cross, Fane, who scored 12,599 runs for Essex, made only spasmodic appearances for the county.

In 1938 at the ripe old age of sixty-three, he got married and had two daughters, the youngest being born when Fane was seventy-seven. He died in 1960 at the age of eighty-five, but in 1956, due to an editorial error, he had read his obituary in *Wisden*, it having been wrongly inserted in mistake for his cousin.

FARNES, KEN

Spotted by Percy Perrin playing for the Gidea Park Club against the Essex Club and Ground, Ken Farnes was given his county debut in 1930. In only his second match he took five for 36 against Kent at Southend. His victims included the great Frank Woolley, caught by Jack Russell at slip first ball, Les Ames and 'Tich' Freeman. That year he went up to Pembroke College, Cambridge, winning a Blue as a freshman the following year and further Blues in 1932 and 1933.

He played in a Test trial in 1932 and was a serious contender for a place on the infamous 'body-line' tour of Australia in 1932-33.

Ken Farnes was a tall, lively fast bowler. Standing 6ft 5ins and weighing 15 stone, he had a superb action. His run was short, only eleven strides, but he could move the ball both ways, bringing it down from such a great height that he was able to get it to lift sharply off the pitch, making it difficult for batsmen to time their strokes.

In 1934 Farnes made his Test debut against Australia at Trent Bridge, taking five wickets in each innings to become the third bowler after Martin and Richardson to take ten wickets in his first Test against Australia.

He missed much of the 1935 season through injury but returned the following summer to take 61 wickets in just eleven County Championship matches. Chosen to tour Australia in the winter of 1936-37 with Gubby Allen's side, he produced his best Test bowling figures of six for 96 in Australia's total of 604 in perfect batting conditions.

Injuries again hampered his progress in 1937 but the following summer he was back to his best, taking 107 wickets at 18.84 runs apiece including eight for 43 for the Gentlemen against the Players at Lord's. That season also saw him chosen as one of *Wisden*'s Five Cricketers of the Year. In 1939 he scored the only hat-trick of his career against Nottinghamshire and had taken his tally of first-class wickets for Essex to 367 when war broke out.

In 1940 Ken Farnes joined the RAF and was sent to do his training in Canada. Within four weeks of his return to England he was killed when the plane he was piloting crashed. He was only thirty years of age and his death was a great blow to both Essex and England cricket.

In June 1954, a memorial in the shape of a scoreboard at the Gidea Park Ground, Romford was dedicated by the Bishop of Chelmsford to Kenneth Farnes, one of the fastest bowlers of all-time and the leading amateur bowler of the 1930s.

FASTEST HUNDRED

In 1975, Robin Hobbs scored 100 against the Australians at Chelmsford in just 44 minutes. It was the fastest hundred for fifty five years. He hit seven sixes and 12 fours and his second fifty took only 12 minutes. It was, at the time, the fifth fastest ever recorded in first-class cricket. It was most certainly the fastest by any Essex player and the fastest conceded by any touring team. However, Essex lost the match by 98 runs and Hobbs was surprisingly left out of the team for the next match at Northampton.

FATHER AND SON

There have been a number of instances of father and son combinations playing for Essex including England Test cricketer Walter Mead and his son, Harold; Frederick Fane, father of the future Essex and England captain of the same name; Arnold Holcombe Read and his son, 'Hopper', both of whom were Old Wykehamists; and Essex captain Denys Wilcox and his son, John.

Keith Fletcher.

FINALS

Essex have appeared in the following limited overs finals:

Year	Opponents	Competition	Result
1979	Surrey	Benson and Hedges	Won by 35 runs
1980	Northamptonshire	Benson and Hedges	Lost by 6 runs
1983	Middlesex	Benson and Hedges	Lost by 4 runs
1985	Leicestershire	Benson and Hedges	Lost by 5 wkts
1985	Nottinghamshire	Nat West Trophy	Won by 1 run
1989	Nottinghamshire	Benson and Hedges	Lost by 3 wkts
1996	Lancashire	Nat West Trophy	Lost by 129 runs
1997	Warwickshire	Nat West Trophy	Won by 9 wkts
1998	Leicestershire	Benson and Hedges	Won by 192 runs

FLETCHER, KEITH

When he arrived to join the Essex staff, some of the players were practising close catching and noticing his long and rather pointed shoes, they promptly nicknamed him the 'Gnome'. Fletcher made his Essex debut in 1962, having only seen one first-class match. The following season he scored 1,310 runs and was awarded his county cap, although the undoubted potential of his cricket had yet to be fulfilled.

His maiden century came in 1964 when he hit an unbeaten 103 against Lancashire at Old Trafford, quickly followed by 125 in Essex's victory over the touring Australians at Southend. In 1965 he totalled 1,486 runs and in the following summer he scored 1,550 runs, among them a superb 106 against the West Indies at Southend, in which he picked up a glorious six down the leg-side off Wes Hall to take him to his hundred. Also in that summer he took forty-two catches, breaking his own record from the previous season. In 1967 he took six catches in the match against Glamorgan at Brentwood, performing the feat on two further occasions, against Worcestershire and Derbyshire in 1977 and 1978 respectively.

He hit the highest score of his career, 228 not out against Sussex at Hastings in 1968, an innings that gained him his first England cap. It came at Headingley that summer and for the wrong reasons. He had been named in the England Twelve but it was not expected that he would play.

However, Tom Graveney cut his hand opening a can of food and Yorkshire's Phil Sharpe who had not even been in the original squad was called up as standby. It was quite natural that Fletcher should play, but of course the Yorkshire crowd saw it differently – they thought Sharpe should play and as Fletcher dropped three catches and made nought, the Leeds crowd never let up.

After finishing second to Geoff Boycott in the national batting averages of 1971, Fletcher had an outstanding season the following summer and it amazed most Essex followers that he was only chosen for one Test.

At the end of the 1973 season Fletcher was appointed captain of Essex in succession to Brian Taylor. A firm disciplinarian, he earned great respect from the players because of his natural ability and he ended his first season in charge as one of *Wisden's* Five Cricketers of the Year.

His appearances in the England side meant frequent absences from Essex and his century against Pakistan at the Oval in 1974 still remains the slowest, at 458 minutes, in English first-class cricket

In 1979, Fletcher led Essex to the County Championship title for the first time in their history. It was the season in which he produced his career best bowling figures of five for 41 against Middlesex at Colchester.

His leadership qualities prompted the England committee to name him captain of the England party to tour India and Sri Lanka in 1981-82. He was the third Essex player to captain his country. Keith Fletcher was the only England captain to win the toss five times in a six Test series and the first England captain to put the opposition in first in India. He played in fifty-nine Tests for England, seven of them as captain. He hit seven centuries, the highest of them being 216 against New Zealand at Auckland in 1974-75 but probably his best Test innings was the 170 also made against New Zealand at Lord's in 1973.

In 1982, his testimonial raised £83,250, following on from the £13,000 his benefit brought him some nine years earlier.

In 1985, Fletcher was invited to Buckingham Palace to receive the OBE from the Queen. It was an honour thoroughly and richly deserved, reflecting the fortunes of both the man and the county club. By the end of that season, Keith Fletcher had become the first captain to have led a county side to the game's four major honours. At the end of the summer he stood down as captain to enable Graham Gooch to gain experience and to offer advice and take over when Gooch was absent on Test duty.

Fletcher went on to score 29,434 runs for Essex and is now the club's cricket consultant. There have been few greater servants to the county club than the 'Gnome'.

FOOTBALLERS

There have been a number of Essex cricketers who have been footballers of real note. Perhaps the most famous is Sir Geoff Hurst who won forty-nine caps for England, demonstrating his all-round talent with three goals in the 1966 World Cup Final against West Germany – one with his head, one with his right foot and the last with his left. Hurst, who scored 248 goals for West Ham United, including six against Sunderland in 1968-69, later played for Stoke City and West Bromwich Albion.

Another England international who played cricket for Essex was Claude Ashton. The Corinthians utility player made just one appearance for his country against Northern Ireland in 1926.

Charles McGahey was a useful full-back for Tottenham Hotspur, Arsenal, Clapton Orient and Sheffield United and Stan Nichols kept goal for Queen's Park Rangers. Brian Taylor played amateur football for Dulwich Hamlet and later as a professional, and Gordon Barker played on the wing for Southend United.

A number of Essex players appeared in the FA Amateur Cup Final – Sonny Avery for Leyton in 1937, Trevor Bailey for Walthamstow Avenue in 1950 and Doug Insole for Corinthian Casuals in 1956.

FORMATION

The Essex County Cricket Club as we know it today, was formed in 1876 but there are references to matches played in the eighteenth century and the first half of the nineteenth century by Essex teams.

Although a county cricket club was established at Chelmsford around 1860, this does not appear to have lasted long and the present Essex County Cricket Club was formed as a result of a meeting held at the Shire Hall, Chelmsford on 14 January 1876 under the chairmanship of James Round, Member of Parliament for Colchester. It was decided that the

County Ground should be at Brentwood and James Round was appointed captain, a position he held until 1882.

FOSTER, NEIL

On 6 May 1980, Neil Foster was celebrating his eighteenth birthday in Colchester by preparing for his 'A' levels at the Philip Morant Comprehensive School. He had just signed forms for Essex and was no

doubt wondering how the Essex side were doing in their match against Somerset at Ilford, as a virus was decimating the team. Such was Essex's plight that Foster was called to the head teacher's office to be told that he had been included in the side for his first-class debut the following day against Kent.

Kent won the toss and elected to bat. Foster, opening the bowling with John Lever, sent his first delivery racing away for four wides. However, in successive overs he claimed the wickets of England internationals Bob Woolmer and Chris Tavare and later Alan Ealham to finish with three for 51 off 15 overs.

By 1982 Foster was beginning to experience pain in his back and this

Neil Foster.

was diagnosed as a stress fracture of a vertebra. He attempted to cure the problem the same way as Dennis Lillee had done – by spending time encased in a plaster corset. Unfortunately for him it did not work and he had to undergo an operation and have steel plates inserted to hold the crack together. However, by the end of May the following season, he had made an amazing recovery and after a summer of fast bowling and hard hitting, he was awarded his county cap. During the course of the season, playing against New Zealand, he gained the first of his twenty-nine England caps.

Foster had a high bowling action which allowed him to extract awkward bounce. When the ball was swinging he could command some useful movement away from the right-hander through the air, getting close to the stumps. When the pitch was receptive to movement, rather than to the atmosphere, he banged it down on the seam. He had enough pace to make all the top-class batsman hurry their shots and could still beat them for speed.

In Madras in 1984-85 in the fourth Test, he took 11 for 163, a match-winning performance achieved in unhelpful conditions against a strong Indian batting side. In 1987 he produced his best bowling figures both in the County Championship and at Test level. He took seven for 33 against Warwickshire at Chelmsford and eight for 107 against Pakistan at Headingley.

In 1990, Foster was the leading wicket taker in the country with 94 wickets at a cost of 26.61 runs each and was named as one of *Wisden's* Five Cricketers of the Year. He also captained Essex for the first time against Glamorgan at Southend but the highlight of his season must surely have been his maiden first-class hundred. It was in a match against Leicestershire and came up in 83 minutes off 81 balls and contained five sixes and eight fours. The following summer Foster was again in fine form, his 91 wickets including career best figures of eight for 99 against Lancashire at Old Trafford.

Sadly, injuries then began to take their toll and at the end of the 1993 season, after he had taken 724 first-class wickets, Neil Foster was forced to retire.

FREEMAN, JOHN

The brother of Kent's 'Tich' Freeman, he made his Essex debut in 1905 and soon made a reputation for himself as a most attractive stroke-maker. This, coupled with his wicketkeeping, made him an important member of the Essex side.

In 1911 he had the unusual distinction of sharing with 'Bob' Carpenter in century partnerships in each innings of the match with Surrey at Leyton, ending the summer with two centuries in a total of 841 runs. He continued to make progress over the next few seasons, his adventurous style exciting the crowds.

John Freeman returned after the First World War as impressive as ever. He was by this time thirty-five and had lost important years to the fighting. In 1919 he was at his prime, hitting exactly 1,000 runs. In 1921, in the match against Derbyshire at Leyton, Freeman found himself to be the only professional in the Essex side that day. Later that summer he hit the highest score of his career, 286 against Northamptonshire. It took him slightly under seven hours to reach this total and he went on to score 1,000 runs for the second time.

For a man of forty-two years of age Freeman had a remarkable season in 1926, scoring 1,958 runs at an average of 41.65, hitting six centuries. Also this season, in the match against Middlesex, he and Russell scored 184 out of 203 made from the bat in Essex's first innings.

After giving way to Lawrie Eastman's younger brother George behind the stumps, Freeman, who had scored 14,507 runs and claimed 276 victims – 230 caught and 46 stumped – decided to retire at the end of the 1928 season.

G

GIBB, PAUL

In his first year at Cambridge University, Paul Gibb made his debut for his home county, Yorkshire, scoring 157 not out against Nottinghamshire for whom Harold Larwood and Bill Voce were the opening bowlers. After playing 36 times for Yorkshire as an amateur and captaining their pre-war Jamaican tour, he dropped out of first-class cricket on his return from Australia in 1947.

His engagement by Essex as a professional in 1951 marked an important step in the economic and social side of cricket history for he was the first University Blue to turn professional.

After making 99 against Kent, he quickly followed it with 107 made against his former county, Yorkshire, at Brentwood. Paul Gibb had an impressive first season for Essex, scoring 1,330 runs and hitting four centuries. One of his best innings came in the return match against Kent at Blackheath as he and Horsfall put on 343 for the third wicket – a new Essex record. Gibb scored 141 and along with Horsfall was later presented with a scorecard printed on silk to commemorate this record. In 1952, Gibb scored 1,519 runs and shared in a new second wicket stand for Essex as he and Sonny Avery put on 294 against Northamptonshire. His aggregate of victims behind the stumps was 87 made up of 69 caught and 18 stumped and put him at the head of English wicketkeepers.

Sadly, a series of injuries began to take their toll and at the end of 1956, after scoring 6,328 runs and claiming 339 victims behind the stumps, he decided to retire. He had represented England on eight occasions and had a batting average of 44.69. In his first Test against South Africa he scored 93 and 106 and in his final Test of that series he made 120.

Paul Gibb had an enormous appetite, with a special liking for ice cream, yet his slender figure was never affected by the large amount of food he ate. He used to travel the country in a small van – this contained most of his belongings and was often his sleeping accommodation.

On his retirement from first-class cricket he became an umpire and in 1977 he arrived at the Centenary Test at Melbourne in a wig and contact lenses and went unrecognised by his many former colleagues. At the time of his death, Paul Gibb was a bus driver in Guildford.

GLAMORGAN

Founded in 1888, Glamorgan have won the County Championship on three occasions, 1948, 1969 and 1997. The county also won the Sunday League in 1993.

Trevor Bailey had two outstanding games against the Welsh county in 1950. At Brentwood the England all-rounder took seven for nought in the space of 31 balls and in the return match at Newport, he performed the hat-trick, his victims being Pleass, Hever and Don Shepherd.

One of the most exciting games in Glamorgan's championship-winning season of 1969 occurred against Essex at Swansea. South African Lee Irvine hit his only century for Essex, 109, and with Brian Taylor scoring 70 they took Essex to a first innings lead of 95. Glamorgan, of course, were desperate to win the game, so Tony Lewis's declaration left Essex just under two hours to get 190 for victory. The county went boldly for the runs but though they maintained the necessary scoring rate, wickets fell at regular intervals. When the last over arrived, Essex wanted seven to win with two wickets remaining. Singles were taken off each of the first three deliveries sent down by Roger Davis but off the fourth, Barker was beaten and stumped. With the last ball about to be bowled, Essex, with their last pair East and Lever at the wicket, wanted three to win. Lever slashed wildly at Davis and the ball flew to third man where Wheatley picked up and threw as Lever turned for the second run which would have tied the match. Sadly, the Essex paceman was beaten by yards and Glamorgan had won by one run.

GLOUCESTERSHIRE

Gloucestershire,founded in 1871,won the unofficial County Championship in 1874, 1876 and 1877 and were joint champions in 1873. Since 1930, the county has finished second in the championship on six occasions.

Gloucestershire have had four one-day successes, winning the Gillette Cup in 1973, the Benson and Hedges Cup in 1977 and 1999 and the Nat West Trophy also in 1999.

In Essex's first confrontation with Gloucestershire at Leyton in 1898 the home side were dismissed for 128, with W G Grace taking seven for 44. Gloucestershire totalled 231 with Grace hitting a masterly 126. After Essex had scored 250 in their second innings, it left Gloucestershire requiring 148 for victory. Charles Kortright dismissed both openers without a run on the board but Gloucestershire recovered to end the day on 81 for three. Early on the last day, with Grace on 49, he edged Kortright to wicketkeeper Russell only to be given not out. Finally Kortright uprooted the Doctor's middle stump, finishing with seven for 57 (match figures of 12 for 98) but Gloucestershire won the match with the last pair at the wicket.

In 1901, Charles McGahey became the first Essex player to score a hundred in each innings when he made 114 and 145 not out in the drawn game against Gloucestershire at Leyton.

Stan Nichols had an outstanding match against Gloucestershire in the 1938 match at Bristol, scoring 159 out of Essex's total of 553 and having match figures of 15 for 165 including nine for 37 in the first innings.

The 1959 meeting at Leyton was tied, Gloucestershire failing by one run to make the 212 needed for victory. During the course of the game, Doug Insole, who later in the season was appointed a Test selector, made 177 not out at almost a run a minute.

In 1978, Mike Proctor's 203 took Gloucestershire to 350 for six but Essex responded with 350 for three. Proctor eventually set Essex 303 to win in a little over three hours. Norbert Phillip was in sparkling form and after reaching his hundred in 112 minutes he was out for 134 with just three balls of the match remaining, but only two runs were required and Lever scored them off the next ball to give Essex victory by two wickets.

GOOCH, GRAHAM

When Graham Gooch first joined Essex, he was a batsman who kept wicket and actually went on a Young England tour to the West Indies as Number 2 wicketkeeper to Gloucestershire's Andy Stovold.

After making his first team debut in 1973, he slowly began to make a

51

Graham Gooch, who is Essex's leading run-getter of all time with 30,701 runs at an average of 51.77, also played in 118 Tests for England, scoring 8,900 runs at 42.58.

name for himself in the Essex middle-order, hitting the first of 94 centuries for the county against Leicestershire at the end of the 1974 season.

He began the 1975 season in superb form. He hit 100 against Kent, 85 against Lancashire and 90 against Nottinghamshire and was selected for the MCC in their match against Australia at Lord's, hitting a sparkling 75. He was awarded his county cap and his belligerent style also brought him a well-earned place in the England team for the first Test at Edgbaston where he made a pair. He played again at Lord's but did not do enough for the selectors to consider him for the remainder of the series and he spent the next couple of seasons in rehabilitation, though he did rediscover his lost confidence sufficiently to be chosen for England's one-day side in 1976.

In 1978 he began to open the innings for Essex and was a great success. He scored 129 against Northamptonshire, helping Ken McEwan add 321 to break the Essex second wicket record. He won back his England place and in the three Tests against New Zealand he was his country's leading batsman with an average of 63.33.

When Essex won the County Championship in 1979, Gooch gave the team an attacking look right from the start. In the Benson and Hedges Final against Surrey, he played a magnificent innings of 120 – the first of a run of successes in Lord's finals that he was to maintain.In 1979-80, still seeking that elusive first Test century, he was run out for 99 at Melbourne.

At the beginning of the 1980 season he hit the first double-hundred of his career – 205 against Cambridge University. In the second Test at Lord's he hit his maiden Test century against the West Indies, by scoring a magnificent 123 out of the first 165 runs – he had already made 1,000 runs in Test cricket prior to his first century. In 1980-81 he toured the West Indies and was by far the most successful of the English batsmen, scoring 116 at Bridgetown and 153 at Kingston to average 57.50 in the series.

In 1982 in the Benson and Hedges Cup zonal match at Hove, Gooch hit the Sussex attack for 198 not out, the highest score made in a one-day competition in England. He also equalled the county record for five catches in an innings against Gloucestershire at Cheltenham (six in the match also to equal the record). The following summer Essex scored 310 for five against Glamorgan at Southend, Gooch scoring 176. Both figures established new John Player League records. He also made a decision to lead a rebel tour to South Africa and a three-year suspension kept him out of the national side until the 1985 home series with Australia.

His batting in 1984 was absolutely brilliant. Captaining the Essex side because Keith Fletcher was injured, he hit the second double century of his career, 220 against Hampshire at Southampton. He was the first man that season to reach 2,000 runs, scoring 2,559, the highest by an Essex player in a season.

In 1985, Gooch hit 171 off 155 balls in the John Player League against Nottinghamshire to set up a record opening partnership of 239 in 38 overs. He also hit 202 in the championship fixture at Trent Bridge and 91 against the same county in the Nat West Final at Lord's as he and Brian Hardie put on 202 for the first wicket. He scored 487 runs (average 54.11) against Australia with a top score of 196 at the Oval. He had a successful benefit, realising £153,906, and at the end of the season replaced Keith Fletcher as captain.

Under his leadership in 1986, Essex won the County Championship for the third time in four years and the fourth time in eight years. In 1988 he hit his highest score in the championship, 275 against Kent at Chelmsford, and later in the summer was appointed captain of England. The following year he ended the season with the highest Sunday League average of 95.66 but in 1990 his achievements were to be even more phenomenal. He topped the national batting averages, scoring 2,746 runs at 101.70 including a dozen centuries and a highest score of 215 against Leicestershire. Against India he scored 752 runs at an average of 125.33. In the opening Test he hit 333 off 485 balls, the innings lasting 627 minutes and containing three sixes and 43 fours. Then, for good measure, he hit 123 in the second innings. Gooch, who is Essex's leading run getter of all time with 30,701 runs at an average of 51.77, also played in 118 Tests for England, scoring 8,900 runs at 42.58.

GREEN, CHARLES

Learning the game at Uppingham, he was one of the first men who earned that school any cricket reputation. He went on to Cambridge and played in the University XI from 1865 to 1868, captaining the side in his last year. He first played county cricket for Sussex in 1868 but for ten years or so after was a regular member of the Middlesex side and one of the most exciting amateurs in the land.

In 1871, playing for the Gentlemen against the Players at the Oval, he scored 57 not out in what was considered to be one of his best innings. He made his last 27 runs from just seven strokes, winning the game for his side with just three minutes to spare.

In 1882 he joined Essex and became captain the following year when he and F H Stevens added 129, the first large stand for the new county club, for the sixth wicket against Northamptonshire at Wellingborough. It was Charles Green who decided that a move away from Brentwood would be in the best interests of the county club. He was a determined man, eager to put the club on a professional basis, and he showed great vision in pushing for the ground at Leyton.

In 1888 he gave way to Lucas as captain but remained chairman and played a prominent part in directing the county through the troubles that lay ahead. Along with Borradaile, it was Green who was to save the club from extinction over the next few years. However, this Father of Essex cricket became bitterly disappointed by the trend towards the importation of overseas players and the lack of support afforded to the county. He resigned as chairman but accepted the position of president and his last act was typical of the man – he paid off the club's debts of £400 so the new regime could start with a clean sheet.

Charles Green was a director of the Orient Steamship Company and was president of the MCC in 1905. His contribution to Essex County Cricket Club is immeasurable, without him it would not have continued.

GREENSMITH, BILL

Although he made his first-class debut for Essex in 1947 against Gloucestershire, it was some four years later before Bill Greensmith, a Yorkshire-born leg-spinner, fulfilled his early promise. In the summer of 1951 he took 46 wickets in the County Championship.

The following year he began to show real potential as an all-rounder. Batting at Number 10 he hit a quick-fire 79 before destroying Leicestershire with a spell of six for 44 in their second innings. In fact, the first five wickets of this spell were taken in 31 balls without a single run being taken off him. Essex won the game by 107 runs.

The following summer, Greensmith hit his maiden first-class century, 138 not out, but it was his leg-breaks and googlies that were causing the problems for many top batsmen and in 1955 he took 84 wickets at 26.42 runs each. In 1956 he enjoyed another good season as an all-rounder, taking 80 wickets at 21.07 each and scoring 544 runs. He missed several matches through injury the following season but still claimed 63 victims. After a disappointing summer in 1958 in which he was left out of the side, he bounced back in 1959 and turned in some creditable performances including six for 40 in the 21 run win over Sussex at Brentwood.

He continued to produce good performances with both bat and ball in 1962, hitting 764 runs and capturing 77 wickets. His best performance with the ball came in the match against Lancashire at Aigburth when he took seven for 59, Essex winning by 28 runs.

In his testimonial year of 1963, Greensmith suffered the fate of so many Essex beneficiaries and lost his place in the side early in the season through ill-health. When he did reappear, his bowling form had deserted him and at the end of the season Greensmith, who had scored 8,042 runs at 20.05 and captured 720 wickets at 28.76 runs apiece, announced his retirement.

H

HAMPSHIRE

Founded in 1863, Hampshire have twice won the County Championship, first under the enthusiastic captaincy of Colin Ingleby-Mackenzie in 1961 and again in 1973, by which time their captain was Richard Gilliat. The county have won the Sunday League on three occasions, in 1975, 1978 and 1986; the Benson and Hedges Cup in 1988 and 1992; and the Nat West Trophy in 1991.

In 1895, Hampshire defeated Essex at Southampton by 171 runs but not before Walter Mead had taken eight for 67 and nine for 52. This bowling performance is still the Essex record for the most wickets in a match. Five years later, Hampshire were Essex's opponents when Mead had the best bowling figures of his career, capturing nine for 40.

In the match against Hampshire at Leyton in 1922, Essex needed 181 to win on a wicket of uneven bounce and were 16 short of victory with Jack O'Connor on 99. After reaching his hundred with a single, he hit successive fours in the next over to clinch victory. His 111 not out from an Essex total of 183 was a masterly innings.

The match against Hampshire at Southampton in 1964 was affected by rain. After three declarations, Essex were set to make 201 in 138 minutes at a rate of 85 runs an hour. They succeeded in doing so with just eight minutes to spare as Robin Hobbs hit 19 off four successive Derek Shackleton deliveries.

HARDIE, BRIAN

Like his father and brother Keith, Stenhousemuir-born batsman Brian Hardie played for Scotland, making his debut in 1970. The following year he scored a century in each innings in the match against the MCC at Aberdeen but as the match was not regarded as first-class the performance was not recognised. However, it had certainly been noted and he joined Essex prior to the start of the 1973 season.

He came into the public eye after hitting just four runs in 142 minutes against Hampshire at Chelmsford and so establishing an Essex record for the slowest innings. He hit his maiden first-class century at Ilford against Middlesex but it took him more than five hours and he gained a reputation of being a slow, dour Scottish batsman. However he soon refuted it by topping 1,000 runs in each of his first three seasons and making the highest score of his career – 162 against Warwickshire at Edgbaston.

Brian Hardie.

Hardie suffered a loss of form and moved down the order, Gooch becoming the opener, but he showed considerable determination in his efforts to overcome his technical limitations. Few who saw him in those early years would have put money on him making runs at county level for eighteen seasons. He later reverted to opener but it did not matter where Brian Hardie batted, he was a batsman for all occasions and for all positions.

In the match against Somerset at Southend in 1985, Hardie equalled his highest score with 162. He hit 110 in Essex's first championship win in 1986 against Yorkshire, returning to play a fine innings after having broken his hand. That summer, Essex retained the John Player League trophy with perhaps their most important victory coming in the match against Nottinghamshire at Trent Bridge. In this match, Hardie and Gooch set up a new John Player League record opening partnership with a stand of 239 in 38 overs.

Probably Hardie's greatest moment came in the 1985 Nat West Trophy Final against Nottinghamshire. Hardie and Gooch put on 202 for the first wicket, the highest partnership of any Lord's Final with Hardie's share being 110. It was his first century in the 60 over competition, deservedly winning him the Man-of-the-Match award.

'Lager', his long-time nickname, decided to retire at the end of the

1990 season and he made the announcement while riding high in the national batting averages. He was a player with a great sense of humour and the most reliable of county cricketer, with the disconcerting habit of hitting the ball in improbable directions.

HARLOW

For many years Essex have followed the policy of playing around the county and the Sunday League has given them an opportunity to appear at some of the lesser known grounds. Harlow, with its extensive facilities, was almost an automatic choice. In 1969, Worcestershire won by a single run but their victory was due to some hard hitting by a former Essex player, Rodney Cass.

HAT-TRICKS

Johnny Douglas scored the first hat-trick for the county in the match against Yorkshire at Leyton in 1905 and Mark Ilott achieved a hat-trick of lbws against Northamptonshire at Luton in 1995. The following players have all performed the feat for Essex:

Year	Bowler	Opponents	Venue
1905	Johnny Douglas	Yorkshire	Leyton
1907	'Sailor' Young	Leicestershire	Leyton
1914	Bert Tremlin	Derbyshire	Derby
1920	Percy Toone	Kent	Leyton
1921	George Louden	Somerset	Southend
1923	Johnny Douglas	Sussex	Leyton
1924	Augustus Hipkin	Lancashire	Blackpool
1925	Jack O'Connor	Worcestershire	Worcester
1931	Stan Nichols	Yorkshire	Headingley
1935	'Hopper' Read	Gloucestershire	Bristol
1939	Ken Farnes	Nottinghamshire	Clacton
1950	Trevor Bailey	Glamorgan	Newport
1950	Peter Cousens	Combined Services	Chelmsford
1971	Stuart Turner	Surrey	The Oval
1974	Keith Boyce	Warwickshire	Chelmsford
1983	Norbert Phillip	Northamptonshire	Wellingborough
1995	Mark Ilott	Northamptonshire	Luton
1996	Ashley Cowan	Gloucestershire	Colchester
1998	Danny Law	Durham	Chester-le-Street

HIGHEST INDIVIDUAL SCORES

The top individual scores by Essex players are as follows:

343*	Percy Perrin	v Derbyshire at Chesterfield	1904
286	John Freeman	v Northamptonshire at Northampton	1921
277	Charles McGahey	v Derbyshire at Leyton	1905
275	Graham Gooch	v Kent at Chelmsford	1988
273	Jack Russell	v Northamptonshire at Leyton	1921
263	Stuart Law	v Somerset at Chelmsford	1999
248	Jack O'Connor	v Surrey at Brentwood	1934
245	Paul Prichard	v Leicestershire at Chelmsford	1990
245	Percy Perrin	v Derbyshire at Leyton	1912
238*	Jim Cutmore	v Gloucestershire at Bristol	1927

HIGHEST INNINGS

The highest individual score in first-class cricket by an Essex player is Percy Perrin's 343 not out against Derbyshire at Chesterfield in 1904. It is the only triple century made by an Essex player and helped them to a total of 597 in their first innings. He hit 68 fours, the law still existing that a six could only be scored when the ball was hit out of the ground. It was claimed some years later that fourteen of his boundaries would now have been classed as sixes.

Derbyshire, in reply, scored 548 thanks to a fine 229 by West Indian Charles Ollivierre. They then dismissed Essex for 97 in their second innings before going on to win by nine wickets.

HIGHEST TEAM SCORES

Essex's highest score is 761 for six declared against Leicestershire at Chelmsford in May 1990. Paul Prichard, who scored a career-best 245 and Graham Gooch 215, established a new second wicket record partnership with a stand of 403.

Kent made the highest score against Essex in June 1934 when they totalled 803 for four declared at Brentwood with Bill Ashdown scoring 332, Les Ames 202 not out and Frank Woolley 172.

HIPKIN, AUGUSTUS

Augustus Hipkin, or 'Joe' as he was more commonly known, was one of Johnny Douglas's discoveries and arrived at Essex from the Loughton Club. It has been said that Douglas spoiled Hipkin by bullying him, but most people believed it was Hipkin himself who was his own worst enemy because despite his obvious talent, he did not possess the temperament to be a really top-flight spinner.

Perhaps the match between Essex and Middlesex at Leyton in Hipkin's debut season of 1923 best sums up the Hipkin-Douglas relationship. Middlesex had scored 489 and Essex were 137 for six when Douglas and Morris came together. They made a good stand before Franklin (who hit his maiden century) joined Douglas for a ninth wicket stand of 160 in just over two hours.

Middlesex were already using their twelfth man when another injury caused the need for them to borrow Essex's twelfth man, who happened to be 'Joe' Hipkin. Douglas was on 96 when he smashed a delivery towards the leg-side boundary. Hipkin running at full stretch took a brilliant one-handed catch. He went round to the dressing-room to apologise to Douglas who replied: 'You bloody fool Hipkin. I would have broken your neck if you had missed it'.

By 1924, Hipkin had made great strides as a spin bowler and took 116 wickets at a cost of 21.72 runs apiece. He topped the county's bowling averages, his best figures being eight for 71 against Gloucestershire at Bristol. Hipkin also performed the hat-trick against Lancashire at Blackpool where his victims were Len Hopwood, Dick Tyldesley and England wicketkeeper George Duckworth.

Hipkin soon began to show signs of developing into an all-rounder and in 1927 hit two centuries. In fact, there were times during his first-class career when his batting performances almost equalled his ability as a bowler and fieldsman.

In his last season, 1931, Hipkin only took four wickets and at the end of the summer, Essex decided not to renew his contract. He had scored 4,239 runs for the county and captured 518 wickets at 25.82 runs apiece as well as holding 209 catches. He went to Scotland where he met with great success as professional with the Uddingstone and West of Scotland clubs.

HOBBS, ROBIN

Robin Hobbs played his early cricket for Chadwell Heath and represented the Employers Liability Insurance Company before his sixteenth birthday. Against another insurance company he scored a century which gained him a new bat and a meeting with the great Jack Hobbs in his Fleet Street sports shop. This type of performance suggested to his employers that he was a better cricketer than insurance clerk and they offered no protest

Robin Hobbs.

when Robin decided to pursue a career in cricket.

Although recognised as an Essex player, it was a rather belated decision by the county to secure his services for they were well off for spinners. Kent offered him terms but Trevor Bailey, then the Essex secretary and captain, refused to release him and so he joined the Essex staff in 1960 as the ninth spinner. In 1964, Hobbs took 81 wickets with his leg-breaks and he was chosen to tour South Africa with the MCC in the winter months.

Robin Hobbs was one of the last regular leg-spinners in the country and a most brilliant fielder. He made some useful contributions with the bat and made seven appearances for England.

In 1968, Essex were 185 for seven against Glamorgan when Hobbs joined Stuart Turner. Between them they hit 192 in just two hours, Hobbs making his maiden century and going on to take seven wickets. He was not used as often as he should have been in the one-day game, considering that in 1968 he performed the hat-trick against Middlesex at Lord's in the Gillette Cup.

In 1975, Robin Hobbs scored 100 in 44 minutes for Essex against

Australia at Chelmsford. It was the fastest hundred for Essex and the fastest conceded by any touring team.

He retired prematurely after scoring 4,069 runs and taking 763 wickets to pursue a career in commerce and play for Suffolk. He later joined Glamorgan as captain, which is not surprising when one considers his performances with both bat and ball against them.

HONOURS

County Champions	1979	1983	1984	1986	1991	1992
Promotion from Div 2	2000					
Nat West Trophy	1985	1997				
Benson and Hedges Cup	1979	1998				
John Player League	1981	1984				

HUNDRED WICKETS IN A SEASON

Eighteen Essex players have performed the feat of taking 100 or more wickets for the county in a season with Stan Nichols having done so on eleven occasions. The first player to do so was Walter Mead in 1895 when he took 128 wickets at 15.39 runs apiece.

The most wickets taken in a season is 172 by Peter Smith in 1947. The last player to take a hundred wickets for the county was Neil Foster in 1986 when he took 100 wickets at 21.39 runs each.

HUSSAIN, NASSER

England captain, Nasser Hussain, first came to the fore after several impressive performances in youth cricket, when he was selected to tour Sri Lanka with the Young England team. He had a most successful tour, saving his best for the second four-day 'Test' when he scored 170. Over the next couple of years, he mixed second team cricket at Essex with his education at Durham University before making his first-class debut for Essex in 1987.

The following season, Essex captain, Keith Fletcher, left himself out of the Essex side in favour of the 20-year-old Hussain. He did not let anyone

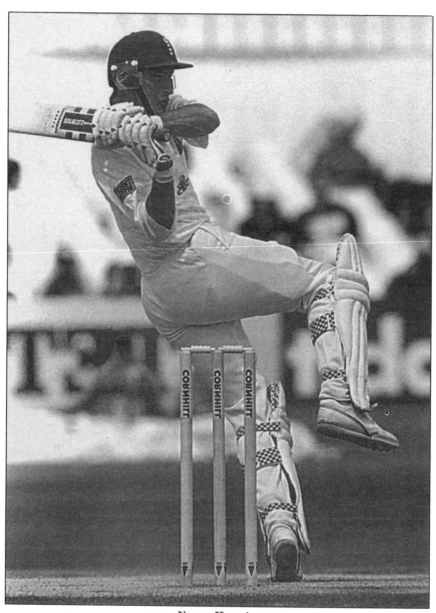

Nasser Hussain.

down, scoring 469 runs at an average of 58.62, including an unbeaten 165 against Leicestershire.

In 1989 he represented the Combined Universities XI in their marvellous Benson and Hedges Cup run, his 118 in the quarter final at Taunton taking his side to within three runs of a remarkable victory. When he rejoined Essex he immediately enhanced his reputation, ending the season with 990 runs at an average of 47.14 and a place in the squad for the final Test match.

In 1990, Hussain made his highest score for Essex, 197 against Surrey at the Oval, and although he went on to take various county attacks apart, it was 1995 before he topped the Essex batting averages, scoring 1,688 runs at 52.75.

Captain of Essex in 1999 after leading the side on numerous occasions due to the frequently injured Paul Prichard, Nasser has scored 11,254 runs for the county at an average of 44.13. At the time of writing, he has appeared in fifty seven Tests and has led England to series victories over the West Indies, Pakistan and Sri Lanka.

ILFORD

Valentine's Park is one of the largest and most attractive parks on the east of Greater London. The Essex county side first played there in 1923 against the West Indians and followed this with games against Somerset and Sussex in 1924 but it was not until 1935, after the removal of the bowling green, that the Ilford Cricket Week was established.

The ground is not really notable for outstanding performances but it was here that Ray Smith flayed the South African bowlers for a century in 70 minutes. One of the most exciting finishes to a game was in the early 1960s when Northamptonshire, with one over to go, were heading for a win. They lost three wickets in the last over and were beaten by two runs.

Valentine's Park was the first ground to stage a County Championship match on a Sunday, when Essex played Somerset in 1981.

ILOTT, MARK

Mark Ilott made his Essex debut in 1988 after playing Minor County cricket for Hertfordshire, for which he is the youngest player to represent that county. After some impressive performances, the left arm medium pace bowler was selected to go on the England 'A' tour of Sri Lanka.

On his return he was playing for Essex against Nottinghamshire in a Sunday League game at Trent Bridge when he felt a shooting pain in his back. Completing his eight-over spell straight off, he retired in agony to the pavilion. A stress fracture of the back was diagnosed but surgery was put off and rest prescribed. However, after a six-week lay-off, the only result was more agony when Ilott attempted to bowl in the Essex second team nets. In August 1991 he went into hospital for an operation and a pin was inserted into his spine. It was a remarkable success and in April 1992 he took the new ball again for Essex. His 62 wickets helped Essex win the County Championship and the following summer he won the first of his five caps for England when he played against Australia at Trent Bridge. He also topped the Essex bowling averages with 48 wickets at 28.10, a feat he achieved on five occasions with a best of 76 wickets at 22.15 runs apiece in 1995.

Also in that year Ilott performed the hat-trick in the match against Northamptonshire at Luton with all of his victims being lbw and finished with career-best figures of nine for 19. A great servant of Essex cricket, 'Ramble' has now taken 507 first-class wickets for the county at an average of 27.63.

INDIA

Essex beat India by seven wickets in the 1936 meeting at Brentwood. Jim Cutmore and Peter Smith both scored centuries as they put on 214 for the eighth wicket. Amarneth scored centuries in both innings for the tourists but was sent home later in the tour for alleged indiscipline.

In 1946 at Southend Essex scored 301 before dismissing India for 138 with Ray Smith taking six for 56. The home side then declared their second innings closed at 201 for three with Harry Crabtree hitting 118. India, left to score 367, won in the last over with their last pair at the wicket.

There was another exciting finish in 1951. Essex bowled out India for 195 with Ray Smith having figures of six for 36. The county then scored 410 with Doug Insole hitting a superb 116. The Indians followed this with a second innings score of 368 for six declared, leaving Essex to score 154 in just 78 minutes. Under the leadership of Doug Insole, the county never shirked a challenge and finished ten runs short on 144 for nine.

INSOLE, DOUG

Doug Insole played his early cricket when he was at Cambridge and in 1947, after the university term, he appeared for Essex in their remaining games. At the end of the summer he had scored 1,237 runs including his first century for the county of 109 not out against Lancashire at Clacton. In 1949 after captaining Cambridge, he returned to Essex where he topped the batting averages with 850 championship runs at an average of 65.38. In that season he hit the highest score of his career, an unbeaten 219 against Yorkshire in a drawn game at Castle Park, Colchester.

In 1950, Insole was appointed joint captain of Essex with Tom Pearce. The step was taken initially to give him the benefit of Pearce's experience before he took over control in June of that year. Also that summer he made his England debut, appearing in the third Test against the West Indies at Trent Bridge. Insole also hit 106 for Essex against Warwickshire in what was the first televised championship match.

Doug Insole.

Over the next few seasons Insole headed the county's batting averages before having the best season of his career in 1955. He scored 2,427 runs, more than anyone else in the country, hitting nine centuries. He scored two of them, 111 and 118, in the same match against Kent at Gillingham and hit an unbeaten 114 against Nottinghamshire at Southend before lunch. He scored 129 against the South Africans at Colchester and was selected for the fourth Test at Headingley. He also captained the Gentlemen against the Players at Lord's and was chosen as one of *Wisden's* Five Cricketers of the Year..

Insole had gained his Blue for football and appeared for Corinthian Casuals in the 1956 FA Amateur Cup Final at Wembley against Bishop Auckland.

In 1956 he was again in tremendous form, scoring 1,988 runs at an average of 41.41. He was the first batsman in the country to reach 1,000 runs, yet made just one Test appearance against the Australians. He was, however, part of the side to tour South Africa, going as Peter May's vice-captain. He was chosen for his one customary Test match – this after he had returned from South Africa and topping England's Test match batting averages. He represented his country on nine occasions, his top score of 110 not out coming at Durban in the third Test of that 1956-57 tour.

During the summer of 1959, Insole was appointed a Test selector, which meant that he played in fewer matches for Essex. At the end of the following season, after leading Essex to sixth place in the championship, he announced his decision to resign the captaincy to concentrate on his business interests.

As captain, Insole led from the front. He believed in playing attractive cricket and his Essex side twice won the *News Chronicle's* Bright Cricket Table. He was always willing to issue or accept a challenge and every year was among the country's leading batsmen, scoring 20,113 runs for Essex at an average of 38.67.

On his retirement from the first-class game at the end of the 1963 season, he continued to give great service to both Essex and the sport in general. He has been a Test selector, chairman of the TCCB, an MCC committee member and the manager of two tours to Australia.

This unconventional batsman with a wonderful eye was awarded the CBE for his services to the game and after serving as chairman of Essex County Cricket Club for a number of years, he is now its president.

IRANI, RONNIE

Bolton-born all-rounder Ronnie Irani's first-class debut for Lancashire was in 1990 but over the next four seasons he made just a handful of appearances. He therefore decided to try his luck with another county and he joined Essex for the 1994 season.

In his first full campaign he scored 882 runs at 40.09 and he took 26 wickets at 29.11. Also during that summer he hit his maiden first-class century, scoring 119 runs against Worcestershire at New Road.

In 1995, Irani scored 1,135 runs at 37.83 and although his bowling proved a little expensive, he picked up his first five-wicket haul, taking five for 62 against Kent at Canterbury. In 1996 he improved his bowling figures by taking five for 27 against Nottinghamshire at Chelmsford and was chosen to play for England against India at Edgbaston. In 1997 he hit his then highest score of 123 against Hampshire at Chelmsford. He was

Ronnie Irani.

appointed vice-captain to Nasser Hussain the following year and although the county finished at the bottom of the championship table, Irani had a good season, scoring 968 runs at 32.26 and taking 40 wickets at 33.70 runs apiece. In 1999 Irani, who was recalled to the England side for the deciding Test against New Zealand, topped the Essex bowling averages with 46 wickets at 21.30 and he hit 129 against Somerset at Bath, the highest score of his career.

Appointed captain for the season of 2000 Irani, who has scored 7,133 runs and taken 246 wickets, led Essex back to the First Division of the County Championship with promotion on the final day of the season.

K

KENT

Founded in 1859, Kent have won the County Championship on six occasions, four times in the golden age of cricket – 1906, 1909, 1910 and 1913 and twice more recently, in 1970 and 1978. They are a consistently successful one-day side and have won nine trophies – four Sunday Leagues in 1972, 1973, 1976 and 1995; three Benson and Hedges Cups, 1973, 1976 and 1978; and two Gillette Cups,1967 and 1974.

In the 1776 meeting between Essex and Kent at Tilling Fort there was a dispute over the qualification of one of the Kent players. The game ended in a riot, resulting in the deaths of the sergeant in charge of the fort, a soldier and one member of the Essex side. Although there are doubts about the authenticity of this tale when the two counties met again at Swanscombe in 1787, relationships still appear to have been strained. Essex won by an innings and Kent refused to drink with their conquerors.

When Essex entertained Kent at Leyton in 1900, Charles McGahey scored 142. He was a hard driver of straight deliveries and in that match drove the ball back so hard that he fractured his partner's arm. In that innings against Kent, he helped Percy Perrin put on 323, setting up what was at the time a world record for the third wicket.

The following year, 'Bob' Carpenter in his benefit season became the first professional to score a hundred in each innings, hitting 127 and 104 against Kent.

In 1934, Kent scored 803 for four, the highest score against the county. wicketkeeper Tommy Wade had an outstanding game behind the stumps in the 1938 match against Kent at Colchester. Kent scored 742 yet Wade only conceded two byes and the first of these did not appear until the score had reached 626.

In 1957, Essex opener, Gordon Barker, helped Dickie Dodds put on 159 before lunch in the match against Kent at Clacton. Four years later he hit the highest score of his career, 181 not out in the 166 run win at Colchester, including getting to his hundred before lunch.

KNIGHT, BARRY

Having played representative cricket for London Schools and South of England Schools at the age of sixteen, Barry Knight was invited to a pre-season 1st XI practice at Chelmsford. He was so impressive with the bat that Trevor Bailey offered him a contract without seeing him bowl.

In 1959 he just missed the double by five runs, scoring 995 at an average of 27.63 and capturing 101 wickets at 23.56 runs each. Not surprisingly, he was awarded his county cap.

Injuries kept Knight out of the side for the latter stages of 1960 but his bowling was of such a high quality that he still captured 88 wickets. In 1961, with 1,148 runs and 89 wickets, the double still eluded him but the following summer he achieved it, scoring 1,689 runs at 34.46 and taking 100 wickets at 24.05 runs apiece. Along with Roger Luckin he put on 206 against Middlesex to equal the 1923 Essex sixth wicket record.

His performances led to him being chosen by the MCC for their close season tour of Australia and New Zealand. In the first Test against the Kiwis at Auckland, Knight and Peter Parfitt put on 240 for the sixth wicket. This is still an English record in all Tests.

In 1963 Knight had an excellent summer, performing the double for the second successive season. He scored 1,578 runs and took 140 wickets. The following year, after yet again completing the double, he won the Carling single wicket competition, beating Northamptonshire opener Colin Milburn in the final at Lord's. The following season, despite it being a wet one, Knight again performed the double, becoming the only first-class cricketer to achieve the feat. At the end of the season he was presented with a cheque for 100 guineas and a clock by the Essex club's committee in recognition of his achievement.

Following the appointment of Brian Taylor as captain at the end of the 1966 season, Knight, who had scored 8,798 runs and captured 761 wickets, decided to leave the club and joined Leicestershire midway through the 1968 season.

On leaving the first-class game in England, he emigrated to Australia, continuing to play a high standard of grade cricket with the Mosman club in Sydney. Cricket is still the centre of his life, as he is now manager of a highly successful cricket school.

KORTRIGHT, CHARLES

Charles Kortright played his early cricket for Brentwood and was soon a success, taking 89 wickets at a cost of just six runs apiece in 1889. His performances attracted Essex and he was invited to play against Leicestershire at Leyton. He was only allowed to bowl two overs at the end of the match but he captured a wicket, that of Arnall-Thompson. He then moved to Hythe to learn the brewery trade and played a lot of club cricket in Kent. Resisting the offer to play for the hop county, he returned to Essex and in 1891 made 158 against Hampshire – the highest individual score recorded for Essex at that time.

In 1893, he took eight for 29 and five for 35 as Surrey were dismissed for 54 and 76 respectively. He was, without doubt, one of the season's great successes. He was described as 'fast, very fast' and had been elected a member of the MCC at the beginning of the summer so that he could be considered for the match against the Australians. He was also selected for the Gentlemen against the Players at Lord's.

In the match against Surrey at Leyton in 1895 Kortright had figures of seven for 72, including the wickets of Hayward, Druce, Abel, Lohmann, Read and Street in the space of fifteen balls for just four runs – but Surrey still won by 201 runs.

In 1898, Kortright hit the first of his two first-class hundreds, 112 against Leicestershire, but was still deadly with the ball, taking six for 10 in the space of ten minutes as Essex beat Hampshire with just fifteen minutes remaining. That summer also saw Essex's first confrontation with Gloucestershire at Leyton and a meeting with W G Grace.

Essex were dismissed for 128 with W G taking seven for 44. Gloucestershire totalled 231, with Kortright taking five for 41 and Grace hitting a masterly 126. Essex rallied in their second innings to score 250, leaving Gloucestershire to make 148 to win. Kortright, bowling at his fiercest, dismissed both openers without a run on the board. When Grace had made 49, Kortright had an appeal for lbw turned down and next ball, the Doctor edged the Essex paceman to wicketkeeper Russell, only to be given not out. Finally, he uprooted Grace's middle stump and as the Doctor was leaving, it is said that Kortright muttered: 'Surely you're not going Doctor, there's still one stump standing.' Kortright went on to take seven for 57 but Gloucestershire won the match with the last pair at the wicket.

Between 1895 and 1898, Kortright took 287 wickets for Essex, 206 of them without any assistance from his fielders. After straining his back at home, he missed the entire 1899 season and was never quite the same again, although the following summer he produced his best-ever figures of eight for 57 against Yorkshire at Leyton.

In 1903, Kortright was invited to captain Essex. It was a strange choice for he was now primarily a batsman, occasionally bowling a few overs of leg-spin and pace. After one year in office, he surprised Essex by announcing at the annual meeting that he was standing down as skipper. Kortright played his last game for Essex against Middlesex in 1907, Pelham Warner being the last of his 440 first-class victims.

Kortright was fond of recounting great tales. There was the one about a club match at Wallingford where he reputedly bowled a ball which rose almost straight and went out of the ground without a second bounce thus making him the first man to bowl six byes.

Charles Kortright was most surely the fastest bowler the game has ever known. Why he never played for his country remains a mystery.

L

LANCASHIRE

Founded in 1864, Lancashire have won the County Championship on seven occasions and were joint champions in 1950. They have made their name as one-day specialists, having won the Gillette Cup/Nat West Trophy in 1970, 1971, 1972, 1975, 1990, 1996 and 1998. They won the Benson and Hedges Cup in 1984, 1990, 1995 and 1996 and the Sunday League in 1969, 1970, 1989 and 1998. In 1999 Lancashire were champions of the CGU National League, Division One.

On a wearing wicket at Leyton in 1896, Lancashire were in trouble but when it looked as if they would follow on, leaving Essex to bat last, Fred Bull bowled one ball so wide that it went for four runs. Arthur Mold then decided to hit his own wicket to make sure Lancashire followed on. Hornby, the Lancashire captain, refused to carry on with the game but after Bull apologised for his antics it continued. For the record, Essex won by six wickets.

In 1898, Lancashire were bowled out for 254 and only a last wicket stand between Bull and Mead prevented Essex from following on, as they totalled 169. The red rose county then scored 250, setting Essex 336 to win, a target no side had ever achieved in an inter-county match. However, the Essex twins, Perrin and McGahey, shared in a third wicket stand of 191 and Essex gained a memorable victory.

When the teams met at Colchester in 1928, Lancashire bowled Essex out for a second time at 6.25pm on the second day and needed just two runs for victory. The players had to return the following morning for what turned out to be two balls. George Eastman, Essex's wicket-keeper did not bother to wear pads, Johnny Douglas wore plus-fours and many other Essex players were in ordinary clothes.

In the 1949 meeting at Clacton, Trevor Bailey became only the second Essex player to take all ten wickets in an innings, finishing with 10 for 90. The match against Lancashire at Brentwood in 1951 ended in a tie after Essex had been set 232 to win in 140 minutes. The last over began

75

with Essex's last pair at the wicket and nine runs needed for victory. Bailey hit the first ball for six, then hit a two but in trying for the winning run, he was caught at mid-off.

LAW, STUART

Essex's current overseas player, Stuart Law began his first-class career with Queensland, which he now captains. His consistent performances with the bat led to him winning a Test cap against Sri Lanka at Perth in 1995-96 when he scored an unbeaten 54. Remarkably, it remains his only appearance at this level.

Law joined Essex in 1996 and ended his first season with the county with 1,379 runs at 59.95 and a top score of 172 against Durham at Hartlepool. He had another successful season in 1997, topping the club's batting averages with 1,482 runs at 57.00 and scoring 175 in the match against Leicestershire at Colchester. Not surprisingly he was selected as one of *Wisden's* Five Cricketers of the Year.

After a summer in which he felt he under achieved, although he was certainly restricted by a shoulder injury, he returned to Queensland, recovered full fitness and enjoyed one of his best seasons with the state side. Law was back to his best in 1999. His batting achievements were quite phenomenal and he topped the national averages with 1,833 runs at 73.32. His double century against Somerset at Chelmsford, when he scored 263, set a new personal best, beating the 217 when playing for Queensland against New South Wales. He scored more runs than anyone else in the country and was the first batsman to reach 1,000 first-class runs. Although Essex were to slide into Division Two of both the County Championship and the National Cricket League, Law was in a league of his own with his batting prowess.

Now, after five seasons with Essex, Law has scored 7,194 runs at an average of 58.02. Perhaps the next record in his sights is to score more centuries than anyone else in a first-class season at Essex.

LEICESTERSHIRE

For many years a Cinderella county, Leicestershire, founded in 1879, became a power to be reckoned with after the appointment of Ray Illingworth in 1969. They were the inaugural winners of the Benson and

Hedges Cup in 1972 and also won it in 1975 and 1985. They won the Sunday League in 1974 and 1977 and captured the County Championship title in 1975 and 1996 when they lost only one game.

Leicestershire were Essex's opponents when they played their first first-class match at Leyton in May 1894, the visitors winning by 68 runs. When Essex played Leicestershire at Leyton the following year, Henry Pickett took all ten wickets for 32 runs but still finished on the losing side.

Charles McGahey enjoyed playing against Leicestershire, for in 1897 he made his second hundred of the week, 123, at Leyton. Two years later he missed his century by one run at Grace Road as Essex totalled 673. In 1900 he hit 184 against Leicestershire, his highest score at the time.

Frederick Fane scored 207 against Leicestershire in 1899. It was the first double century to be made by an Essex player.

The 1906 meeting at Southend was a dramatic one. Leicestershire won the toss and elected to bat. Getting off to a flying start with 74 runs in the first three-quarters of an hour, they totalled 303. Essex looked likely to grab a first innings lead but Benskin ended the home side's innings with a hat-trick to give Leicestershire a lead of 23 runs. Buckenham and Douglas bowled well for Essex, reducing Leicestershire to 54 for seven in their second innings before the lower-order batsmen took the score to 107. Needing 131 to win, Essex won with wickets to spare despite play not getting under way until mid-afternoon on the last day.

Against Leicestershire at Chelmsford in 1975 Keith Boyce scored a century in 58 minutes, including eight sixes and seven fours – and had match figures of 12 for 73.

In May 1990, Essex scored their highest total in the County Championship when they rattled up 761 for six against Leicestershire at Chelmsford.

LEVER, JOHN

In his early days at Essex, John Lever showed plenty of promise as a batsman, hitting 91 against Glamorgan at Cardiff after being sent in as a nightwatchman. It was said many times that with a little more application to his batting, he could have become another Trevor Bailey.

Lever was a captain's dream as a bowler. Whatever the conditions or the state of the game, he wanted to bowl. He was a very fit player and was able to keep going for long spells. As a fast-medium left arm bowler, his pace was sharp rather than genuinely quick. He had a long, relaxed run-up, a beautiful body action and a perfect follow through. He had a superb command of line and length which was why he had such a splendid record in limited overs cricket.

By the mid 1970s, John Lever began to attract the attention of the Test

John Lever.

selectors as a bowler of penetration and stamina. He was chosen for the tour of India and Sri Lanka and was later to play in the Centenary Test in Melbourne. In his first game for England at Delhi on that 1976-77 tour, he scored 53 and took seven for 46 – the best bowling performance achieved by any England player on a Test debut. In 1978, Lever topped the 100 wicket mark for the first time, taking 106 wickets at a cost of just 15.18 runs apiece. He was the first Essex bowler to achieve this feat for twelve years and was named as one of *Wisden's* Five Cricketers of the Year. He also won the coveted award among professionals of the Players' Player of the Year. In fact, he won the award a second time, which just goes to show the great esteem that his fellow professionals around the country held for him.

In 1979 he topped the 100 wicket mark again, helping Essex to win their first trophy. The following summer he had his benefit season and from 1982 to 1985, he spent his winters playing for Natal in South Africa.

Despite undergoing minor surgery in 1983, Lever still reached 100 wickets; an achievement that went a long way in helping win the County

Championship. In 1984 he became the first bowler to reach 300 wickets in the John Player competition, beating Kent's Derek Underwood by just 30 minutes. That summer he achieved his best figues, taking eight for 37 on a superb batting track at Bristol as Gloucestershire were bowled out for 90. He was the first player in the country that summer to reach 100 wickets.

He deservedly had a second benefit season in 1989, something only being awarded to the hardiest and best of performers, and it raised £135,596.

Lever, who took 1,473 wickets for Essex, had a rather disappointing last summer with the county. He was involved in the last ball finish in the Benson and Hedges Final against Nottinghamshire and could not play in the Refuge Cup final at the end of the season due to a recurrence of an old back injury.

After leaving Essex he became sports master at Bancrofts School and played Minor Counties cricket for Cambridgeshire, although the county retained his registration for first-class cricket.

John Lever had a great determination and will to win and was the complete professional. Significantly his career coincided with a successful period in Essex's history.

LEYTON

The Leyton ground was bought for £12,000 in 1886 and remained the Essex headquarters until 1933. It was at Leyton that the initial first-class matches were played in 1894.

Perhaps the leading statistic is the stand of 555 for the first wicket by Percy Holmes (224*) and Herbert Sutcliffe (313) for Yorkshire in June 1932. On the first day both batsmen played happily and shortly before lunch on the second day the new record was established. Directly it was reached, Sutcliffe threw his wicket away and the innings was declared closed. As the batsmen returned to the pavilion there was a shocked silence as the scoreboard moved back to 554 and it seemed that a new record had perhaps been missed. Eventually it was found that a no-ball had not been recorded and the new record was safe.

Walter Mead took seventeen Australian wickets, with figures of nine for 136 and eight for 69, in the match at Leyton in 1893 but this feat was not accorded first-class status as at the time the county was playing in the second-class category..

In 1895, Henry Pickett took all ten wickets in an innings for just 32 runs against Leicestershire and two of Johnny Douglas's best all-round feats took place at Leyton. In 1921 he scored 123 not out and took seven for 91 and seven for 65 against Gloucestershire and later scored 210 not out and took nine for 47 against Derbyshire.

Essex returned to Leyton in July 1957 after an absence of 24 years with Denis Compton scoring a magnificent century in Dickie Dodds' benefit match. After that the county returned for a festival week for a good number of years.

LOUDEN, GEORGE

George Louden was a tall, strong pace bowler whose main asset was his accuracy. He had a high, easy action and could bowl very fast. His best season was 1919 when he took 66 wickets with a best of seven for 42 against Lancashire. Between 1919 and 1923 he played on a regular basis for the Gentlemen against the Players in fixtures at Lord's, the Oval, Folkestone and Scarborough. The following season he produced what turned out to be the best analysis of his career when he took eight for 36 against Derbyshire at Southend.

He did not really play a full season, but in the years immediately after the First World War he must have been on the verge of Test selection. Louden worked in an office in the City and could never really spare the time to play cricket regularly or perhaps more honours would have come his way.

In 1921 he performed the hat-trick in the match against Somerset at Southend and the following season headed the bowling averages with 49 wickets in seven matches, including eight for 48 against Sussex. Louden was a superb fast bowler but often he had to bowl for thirty overs on the trot until he was completely exhausted.

Sadly, Louden's career in which he took 415 wickets at 21.84 runs each, was relatively short and brought to an abrupt end by uncertain health. Yet when he died in December 1972, he had reached the age of eighty-seven.

LOWEST

Essex's lowest score of 30 was made against Yorkshire at Leyton in August 1901. In fact, they could only score 41 in their second innings and Yorkshire, who were themselves dismissed for 104, won by an innings. Hirst and Rhodes bowled unchanged in both innings, the former having match figures of 12 for 29. Yet despite this, Essex and recent newcomers Durham, remain the only first-class counties never to have been bowled out for under 30.

Surrey have made the lowest score against Essex, being all out for just 14 at Chelmsford in May 1983. The first day's play was washed out and on the second day Essex totalled 287, leaving Surrey with just an hour to bat. They were dismissed inside 15 overs with Norbert Phillip taking six for 4 and Neil Foster four for 10.

LUCAS, ALFRED

Alfred Percy Lucas was educated at Uppingham School where he was without doubt, H.H.Stephenson's star pupil. It was a debt he never forgot, he was always saying how much he owed his teacher.

On leaving Uppingham in 1874 he was chosen to represent the Gentlemen of the North v the Players of the South at Prince's and, in scoring 48 and 23, played the bowling of Morley and Shaw with great style.

Lucas went up to Clare College, Cambridge where he won his Blue as a freshman and was in the Cambridge XI for four years. His top score in the four matches with Oxford was 74, topping the University averages in 1876 and 1877. He was a regular choice for the Gentlemen in their fixture against the Players, excelling in 1878 with 91 and in 1882 with a fine 107, both matches being played at Lord's.

'Bunny' Lucas had a classic technique and was so positive in his play that he seldom bored the crowd. He carried his bat through a completed innings on three occasions – for Surrey, the MCC and the Gentlemen.

At the Oval in 1880, he shared in a stand of 120 for England's second wicket with W G Grace and it was Test cricket's first century partnership.

After playing for both Surrey and Middlesex, he threw in his lot with

Essex in 1889 with a view to helping his life-long friend, Charles Green.

He made his debut for the county in May 1889 against the MCC at Leyton, scoring a forceful 103 and went on to score a number of centuries, the highest of which was 175 against Hampshire in 1893, before the county played first-class cricket.

On 14 May 1894 he captained Essex in their first match as a first-class county against Leicestershire. Unfortunately the pressures of business prevented him from continuing as Essex captain in 1895 but he stayed with the county until 1907, scoring 3,554 first-class runs at 26.92. His last match in Essex colours against the touring South Africans resulted in him bagging a pair.

M

MCEWAN, KEN

South African-born batsman Ken McEwan was encouraged by former England captain, Tony Greig, to come to England and join the Sussex groundstaff. He played for the Sussex 2nd XI for two summers but there was little hope of him being signed as the south coast county had more than its fair share of overseas players.

In July 1973 Essex invited him to play in a friendly at Perth against Scotland. He did well and was at once offered a three-year contract which he accepted. By the end of his first season, 1974, he had scored more than 1,000 runs and gained his county cap. All this after being given out lbw from the first ball that he faced in the County Championship against Nottinghamshire.

In the match against Sussex at Chelmsford in 1977 he hit the first double century of his career – a chanceless 218. The next Sunday he hit 104 in the

John Player League game against Warwickshire and went on to score 102 and 116 at Edgbaston against the same county. Then, in the next match against Gloucestershire at Southend, he scored an unbeaten 106. He hit eight centuries that summer and was chosen as one of *Wisden's* Five Cricketers of the Year.

Although he continued to score freely in all competitions, his cricket was not just confined to Essex. He played for Eastern Province (1972-1978), Western Australia (1979-1981) and then joined Western Province in 1981, playing for them until the end of the 1986 season.

In 1983 McEwan became the first batsman to reach 1,000 runs and he finished the summer with 2,176 runs at an average of 64.00. Next season he became the first player to reach 2,000 runs with a beautiful unbeaten 189 against Worcestershire. In 1985, when Essex beat Nottinghamshire by one run in the Nat West Trophy Final, it was Ken McEwan's last appearance at a great cricket match. He ended on 46 not out including one tremendous six off a cover drive into the Mount Stand.

After twelve glorious seasons with Essex, in which he scored 18,088 runs at 43.37, Ken McEwan decided to retire to his farm in South Africa. He could, I am quite sure, have gone on for another five years at least but was tired of driving around the country without any prospect of playing Test cricket at the end of it.

MCGAHEY, CHARLES

A natural hitter in club cricket, he first appeared for Essex in 1893 when the county was second-class. McGahey advanced slowly but profited much from practice against professional bowling provided by Charles Green before each season at Leyton. His experience gained in match play also helped and, as his form improved, he became one of the best batsmen of his time.

In 1898 McGahey's name became linked with Percy Perrin following a third wicket stand of 191 against Lancashire. They became known as the 'Essex Twins' as they were of a similar build and were involved in a number of partnerships together.

For many years McGahey, a bachelor, lived at the Three Blackbirds, a public house in Leyton. He had a strong football connection and was a very useful full-back for Tottenham Hotspur, Arsenal, Clapton Orient and Sheffield United. He also captained Middlesex and London representative teams. He was a man noted for his wit and liking the odd drink. In a match against Somerset, McGahey was dismissed quite quickly and on his return to the pavilion, he was asked by a colleague who had missed his dismissal what had happened. 'Bowled first ball by a bugger I thought died 300 years ago – Robinson Crusoe'. The name stuck and R C Roberston-Glasgow was 'Crusoe' ever after.

McGahey's most successful season was 1901 when he scored 1,838 runs at 48.36 and won a place in Archie MacLaren's side to tour Australia. That summer he scored 114 and 145 not out against Gloucestershire, becoming the first Essex player to hit a century in each innings and was chosen as one of *Wisden's* Five Cricketers of the Year.

He hit his highest score of 277 against Derbyshire at Leyton in 1905 before captaining the county from 1907 to 1910. After being replaced as captain by Johnny Douglas, McGahey continued to play for the county and in 1912 he and Perrin put on 312 in three hours for the third wicket against Derbyshire.

McGahey, who scored 19,079 runs and captured 306 wickets, later became the county's official scorer. During this period he recorded Yorkshire's historic opening partnership and was involved in the recount which arrived at the finally accepted 555.

Percy Perrin described him as 'one of the most popular and kindest-hearted players ever seen in first-class cricket'. Certainly no man gave more of his life to Essex cricket than Charles McGahey.

MEAD, WALTER

Walter Mead was born in Clapton but moved to play as professional at Broxbourne Cricket Club. This move, coupled with his residence in Essex, gave him the necessary qualifications to play for that county.

He had been engaged as a bowler at Lord's and even at his medium-pace he could make the ball turn sharply. Probably his most effective delivery was the leg-break although he often hurried the batsmen into their shots. In 1891, his second season with the county, he took nine for 23 against Leicestershire, with eight of his victims being clean bowled. In

1893 he took 17 wickets in a match for the first time with figures of nine for 136 and eight for 69 against Australia.

Mead had his best season in 1895. He took 128 wickets for Essex and had an overall total of 79 wickets, including all first-class matches. It is a record that has not been beaten by an Essex bowler in the past 106 years In Essex's first victory since becoming a first-class county, Mead took five for 64 and five for 62 as well as hitting 33 and 35 not out against Somerset – a great all-round performance from a man who could always be relied upon to get both runs and wickets when they were most needed. That season Hampshire defeated Essex at Southampton by 171 runs but not before Mead had taken eight for 67 and nine for 52, still the Essex record for the most wickets in a first-class match.

Mead rarely performed brilliantly with the bat but he stunned everyone by hitting 119 at Leyton against Leicestershire in 1902. After being named as one of *Wisden's* Five Cricketers of the Year in 1903, Mead asked the Essex committee for an increase in pay for the winter months. His request could not have come at a worse time for the Essex finances were at a low ebb. Mead played for both the MCC and London County in his time away from Essex before returning for the 1906 season. He continued to top the county's bowling averages for the next few seasons, ending his career with 1,472 wickets at 19.30 runs apiece. He was the mainstay of the Essex attack for almost their first two decades in the County Championship.

MIDDLESEX

Founded in 1863, Middlesex won the unofficial county title in 1866 and won ten official championships, their last being in 1993. Middlesex have also won seven one-day competitions – the Gillette Cup in 1977 and 1980; the Benson and Hedges Cup in 1983 and 1986; the Nat West Trophy in 1984 and 1988; and the Sunday League in 1992.

The first Lord's ground, named after Thomas Lord, was the scene of the first cricket match between Essex and Middlesex on 31 May and 1 June 1787. It is believed to be the first match of any importance to be played on any of the Lord's grounds and Middlesex beat Essex by 93 runs.

When Essex met Middlesex at Lord's in 1906, Frederick Fane and

Johnny Douglas added 209 for the first wicket – it was the first opening partnership of more than 200 runs.

Middlesex were the current County Champions when Essex played them at Leyton in 1920. Essex, batting first, could only muster 133 and Middlesex replied with 212. In their second innings, Essex scored 196 leaving Middlesex 118 to win. Johnny Douglas, bowling with great tenacity, had the first six Middlesex batsmen back in the pavilion with the score on 33. Middlesex rallied, Plum Warner scoring 46 and still at the wicket when their last man came out to bat. Douglas bowled the perfect yorker to dismiss him and take Essex to a remarkable four-run win.

At Southend in 1939, Middlesex were Essex's opponents in a match Lawrie Eastman had chosen for his benefit. Eastman, who had batted in every position except Number 11, was forced to bat last as he was suffering from water on the knee. Essex unfortunately lost by five runs but would certainly have won if Eastman had not been injured.

The match at Lord's in 1984 was an exciting affair. The first innings' scores were Middlesex 329 for nine and Essex 364 for seven. When Middlesex were bowled out for 245 in their second innings, Essex needed 211 to win off 33 overs. As dusk was gathering in, most spectators expected the match to peter out in a draw but in spite of wickets falling at regular intervals, each player made a dashing contribution, none more so than Graham Gooch who made an unbeaten 105 as Essex won by four wickets with seven balls to spare.

MOST RUNS

The following batsmen have scored the most runs for Essex:

		Runs	Average
1	Graham Gooch	30,701	51.77
2	Keith Fletcher	29,434	36.88
3	Percy Perrin	29,172	36.19
4	Jack O'Connor	27,819	35.21
5	Jack Russell	23,610	40.91
6	Gordon Barker	21,895	29.15
7	Trevor Bailey	21,460	34.50
8	Doug Insole	20,113	38.67
9	Charles McGahey	19,079	30.57
10	Dickie Dodds	18,565	28.73

MOST WICKETS

The following bowlers have taken the most first-class wickets for Essex:

		Wickets	Average
1	Peter Smith	1,610	26.28
2	Stan Nichols	1,608	21.26
3	Trevor Bailey	1,593	21.99
4	John Lever	1,473	23.54
5	Walter Mead	1,472	19.30
6	Johnny Douglas	1,443	23.32
7	Ray Smith	1,317	30.23
8	Ken Preston	1,155	26.22
9	Ray East	1,010	25.54
10	Lawrie Eastman	975	26.77

N

NAT WEST TROPHY

Essex first reached the final of the Nat West Trophy in 1985. Put in to bat by Nottinghamshire captain Clive Rice, Gooch and Hardie opted for the steady start, the first six overs yielding just six runs. Rice hoped that Richard Hadlee might be able to exploit any early life in the pitch but an edge off Gooch which fell short of the slips was the nearest the New Zealander came to taking a wicket. In fact, it was the nearest anyone came until mid-afternoon by which time, Brian Hardie had smashed his way to an admirable century.

Gooch and Hardie put on 202 for the first wicket – a record for any wicket in an English final – and provided a perfect springboard for a farewell cameo of deftly timed strokes by Ken McEwan. Together with Pringle he put on 77 in the last ten overs, 54 in the last five to leave Essex on 280 for two. Undaunted by the fact that no side batting second had scored 281 in a final at Lord's, Robinson, Broad and Randall kept Nottinghamshire on schedule. However, with 12 overs left, they still required 101. Following a quickfire 22 by Hadlee, Martindale and Randall pushed the ones and twos until, when the last over began, Nottinghamshire needed 18 to win. Such situations have always brought the best out of Derek Randall and he plundered 16 runs off Derek Pringle's first five offerings. Fletcher took a full minute to calm and set his fielders for the final ball. Randall again moved outside his leg stump to hit it on the off, was tucked up and could only clip it to Paul Prichard who pulled down a difficult catch at mid-wicket and give Essex victory by one run.

Essex's next appearance in a Nat West Trophy Final came in 1996. Their opponents, Lancashire, were bowled out for 186 with John Crawley contributing a fine 66. The stage seemed set for Graham Gooch to make an important contribution to what was likely to be his last major match at Lord's. In the event the Essex captain could only watch in dismay as his side slumped to 33 for six. It looked as though he would carry his bat for the princely score of ten when Gallian's first ball trapped him leg-before. Peter Martin and Glen Chapple used the conditions superbly with Chapple finishing with six for 18 as Essex collapsed to 57 all out, the lowest total in any inter-county final.

Essex were back at Lord's the following year where their opponents were Warwickshire. Again they were very much the underdogs but a devastating spell by Ashley Cowan and a tight spell by Ronnie Irani restricted Warwickshire to 170. Essex's opening batsmen, Paul Prichard and Stuart Law, surpassed last year's total of 57 off just six overs. The two batsmen flayed the Warwickshire attack, Donald included, in a partnership of 109 runs from 82 balls. Stuart Law's tenth four in an innings of 80 not out ended proceedings with a monumental 33.3 overs still unbowled.

Essex's Nat West Trophy records include:

Highest innings total	386 for five v Wiltshire at Chelmsford 1988
Lowest innings total	57 v Lancashire at Lord's 1996
Highest individual score	144 by Graham Gooch v Hampshire at Chelmsford 1990
Best bowling performance	5 for 8 by John Lever v Middlesex at Chelmsford 1972
Highest partnership	202 for 1st wicket (Graham Gooch and Brian Hardie) v Nottinghamshire at Lord's 1985

NEW ZEALAND

In May 1927 Essex beat New Zealand at the County Ground, Leyton. The match was made memorable in that, for the first time in the history of the game, as an exploratory venture a commentary on it was being broadcast.

In July 1969, in a low-scoring match at Westcliff, Essex became the first team to beat the New Zealand tourists. However, the outcome was unlikely when Essex stood at 102 for eight in their second innings – only 22 ahead. But then Ray East with 58, and brilliant spin bowling by Robin Hobbs, David Acfield and East, reduced the Kiwis to 61 for nine chasing 113 to win. Although the New Zealanders' last pair put on 36, Essex won by 15 runs.

Essex were also the only team to beat the New Zealanders in 1999. They won by an innings and 40 runs and did so without Test stars Nasser Hussain, Stuart Law, Mark Ilott and Peter Such.

NICHOLS, STAN

Stan Nichols came from farming stock and in his early days he was not even considered a bowler by the village team for which he played. When he was taken on the Essex groundstaff, it was purely as a batsman. It was Percy Perrin who deserves most credit for converting Stan Nichols from a specialist left handed middle-order batsman into one of the best all-rounders of the 1930s.

In 1929, Nichols became the first Essex professional to complete the double, scoring 1,301 runs and capturing 104 wickets. He was to achieve this feat eight times, more than any other Essex player. In 1931, Nichols performed the hat-trick against Yorkshire, his victims being Wilf Barber, Ellis Robinson and Alf Wood.

He had the honour of being selected as one of *Wisden's* Five Cricketers of the Year in 1933, a season in which he was the first player in the land to reach 1,000 runs and 100 wickets.

Nichols, who played for England in fourteen Tests, made an important contribution to the seven wicket defeat of South Africa in 1935, following his figures of four for 35 with a hard-hitting innings of 70. However, the sensation of that 1935 season was the game between Yorkshire and Essex at Huddersfield. The Tykes had not lost a game since August 1934 but were shot out for 31 – at one stage they were 9 for six. Nichols took four for 17 from 6.4 overs and 'Hopper' Read took six for 11. Essex, too, struggled and were 65 for five when Nichols produced a magnificent innings of 146 before falling to a catch by Hutton off the bowling of Bowes. Yorkshire did not fare much better in their second innings, being dismissed for 99 with Nichols taking seven for 37. Without doubt, Nichols' performance of 146 runs, which was 16 more than Yorkshire could total in two innings, and bowling figures of 11 for 54 was the greatest of his career.

In 1938, Nichols enjoyed his finest season, scoring 1,452 runs at 35.41 and taking 171 wickets at a cost of 19.92 runs each. At Gloucester that summer, Essex defeated the home side by an innings and 65 runs, Nichols having an outstanding match. He scored 159 out of Essex's total of 553 and then took nine for 37 and six for 128. At one stage in Gloucestershire's first innings he had figures of five for 6 in five overs.

Nichols was a great-hearted player, scoring 15,736 runs and capturing 1,608 wickets. Though not wishing to infer anything to the detriment of Essex, he would, I am sure, have gained more international honours if he had played for a more fashionable club. His achievements in obtaining eight doubles was an output only exceeded by Rhodes, Hirst, Jupp and Astill.

NICKNAMES

Many players in the club's history have been fondly known by their nickname. They include:

Trevor Bailey	1946-1967	'Boil'
Gordon Barker	1954-1971	'The Great Bark'
Brian Edmeades	1961-1976	'Chanson'
Brian Hardie	1973-1990	'Lager'
Alfred Lucas	1894-1907	'Bunny'
Jack O'Connor	1921-1939	'Laughing Cavalier'
Douglas Read	1933-1935	'Hopper'
Brian Taylor	1949-1973	'Tonker'
Harding Young	1898-1912	'Sailor'

Percy Perrin and Charles McGahey were known as the 'Essex Twins'.

NORTHAMPTONSHIRE

Founded in 1820, Northamptonshire have never won the County Championship, their best performance being second place, a position they have occupied four times. They have won the Gillette Cup in 1976 and in 1992 under the title of the Nat West Trophy, and the Benson and Hedges Cup in 1980.

In the match at Brentwood in 1947, Northamptonshire's first wicket put on 96 before Peter Smith was brought on to bowl. He took five wickets for one run in the space of 15 balls and Northamptonshire were bowled out for 106.

In 1952, in the match at Northampton, Sonny Avery made 224, the highest score of his career, as he and Paul Gibb set up a new Essex second wicket partnership record of 294.

In 1954 Doug Insole, who topped the county's batting averages, came very close to registering a century in each innings in the match against Northamptonshire at Romford. He scored a superb unbeaten 156 in the first innings and as captain he declared the Essex second innings closed with his own score on 92 not out.

NOTTINGHAMSHIRE

Founded in 1841, Nottinghamshire were undoubtedly the strongest team in the country in the late nineteenth century, taking ten unofficial county titles between 1865 and 1886. Since those days they have had occasional successes, taking the championship again in 1907, 1929, 1981 and 1987. They won their first one-day title in 1987 when they captured the Nat West Trophy and followed this up with the Benson and Hedges Cup in 1989 and the Sunday League in 1991.

In 1938 Essex beat Nottinghamshire at Trent Bridge by just 11 runs – this after being bowled out for 58 in the first innings and seeing the home side gain a first-innings lead of 184. Essex's hero was Sonny Avery who hit a magnificent 136 in Essex's second innings.

In 1985, Graham Gooch hit 171 off 155 balls in the John Player League game at Trent Bridge, setting up a record opening partnership of 239 in 38 overs. He also hit 202 in the championship fixture at Trent Bridge. The men from Nottinghamshire must have hated the sight of Gooch that season, for he hit 91 against them in the Nat West Final at Lord's as he and Brian Hardie (110) put on 202 for the first wicket.

O

O'CONNOR, JACK

Jack O'Connor was a right handed batsman and spin bowler, the nephew of 'Bob' Carpenter and the son of John O'Connor who had played nine games for Derbyshire in 1900 as well as appearing for Cambridgeshire.

In 1922, his second season with the county, O'Connor made an unbeaten 102 against Northamptonshire, the first of 71 centuries. Batting with the elegance and freedom that were to become his hallmark over the next sixteen seasons, O'Connor helped Douglas put on 206 for the sixth wicket against Gloucestershire at Cheltenham, a stand that has been equalled but never beaten.

O'Connor claimed a hat-trick at Worcester in 1925, where his leg breaks bowled M K and H K Foster and then gave him a return catch off the bat of Gilbert Ashton. In all matches during the summer of 1926 he scored 1,402 runs and took 93 wickets, thus narrowly missing the double. In 1928 O'Connor reached his highest aggregate to date with 2,256 runs at an average of 47.44 including six centuries,and the following summer his total of 2,288 runs contained nine hundreds. In his 116 against Kent at Folkestone, he scored 92 of his runs in boundaries, eight of them from consecutive scoring strokes.

He played for England on four occasions when a batsman's place in the side was probably at its most competitive. In 1932, O'Connor suffered a bad injury at Old Trafford in the Test trial. He had his finger split by a ball from Harold Larwood and it kept him out of the game for more than a month. It was tragic, as O'Connor had shown outstanding form up to the middle of June, scoring 906 runs in 14 innings. He went on to score 2,077 runs at 44.19 including a superb innings of 237 against Somerset at Leyton. In 1934 he had his best season, scoring 2,350 runs at an average of 55.95, including nine centuries. His top score was 248, made in the match against Surrey at Brentwood.

He continued to top the 1,000 run mark, a feat he achieved in fifteen consecutive seasons. In 1938 he became the first professional to captain Essex when he took charge for the match against Somerset at Chelmsford.

The Second World War ended O'Connor's career, which had seen him score 27,819 runs and take 537 wickets, but he coached, first at Eton and later at Chigwell, and for two seasons in 1946 and 1947 appeared for Buckinghamshire.

Known as the 'Laughing Cavalier', his value to the Essex side was immense. He scored a century against all the other first-class counties and also against both Cambridge and Oxford.

OVERSEAS PLAYERS

Essex have had a number of foreign-born players in their ranks prior to the influx of overseas players in the county game.

As early as 1891 South African Test player, Henry Taberer, turned out in a number of games for the county and in the 1950s Essex had the services of two West Indian Test cricketers. Ken Rickards appeared in one game for the county in 1953 and six years later Dr Bertie Clarke took 58 wickets with his leg-breaks at 23.32 runs each. One of the most popular overseas players to represent Essex was the Barbadian, Keith Boyce, who joined the county in 1966. He gave great service to Essex, scoring 6,848 runs at 22.75 and capturing 662 wickets at 23.72 runs apiece. Another South

Australian Test captain, Allan Border, helped Essex win the County Championship in 1986, heading the batting averages with 1,287 runs at 51.48. He returned to play for the county again two years later, scoring 1,361 runs at 59.17.

African, Lee Irvine, joined Essex in 1968. He played for the county for

Salim Malik.

two seasons, scoring 2,674 runs at an average of 34.72. In 1970, Pakistani batsman Sadiq Mohammed played in one match and the following summer Australian Bruce Francis made his Essex debut. He spent three seasons with the county, scoring 2,962 runs at 38.46.

South African Ken McEwan gave twelve seasons' service to Essex, scoring 18,088 runs at an average of 43.37 and a highest score of 218 against Sussex at Chelmsford in 1977.

Norbert Phillip arrived at Essex in the summer of 1978 and over the next eight seasons, proved himself a more than useful all-rounder with 3,784 runs and 423 wickets.

Other overseas players to represent Essex in recent years have included Salim Malik of Pakistan and Mark Waugh and Michael Kasprowicz of Australia. The county's current overseas player is another Australian, Stuart Law.

OWEN, HUGH

Hugh Glendower Palmer Owen, whose Christan names hint of his Welsh extraction, was born at Bath in May 1859. He was educated privately and later at Corpus Christi, Cambridge. Yet despite doing great things for his college, he was given little chance for the University side and did not get a Blue.

At one time Owen was qualified to play for three counties – Somerset by birth, Derbyshire by residence and Essex by family home. Fortunately he chose the latter. He first played for Essex in 1880 but his career as a county player really dates from 1885 when he scored an unbeaten 64 against Hertfordshire and 52 against Northamptonshire. In 1887, playing for Trent College where he was a master for nine years, he hit five centuries and totalled 1,809 runs for the season. In the following summer he made 35, 104, 205, 31, 119, 55 and 23 in successive innings between 16 June and 19 July and was dismissed only once.

In 1889 Owen scored 1,839 runs and took 108 wickets with his right arm medium-paced deliveries and hit his highest score for Essex, 153 against Leicestershire at Leyton. Owen had gone in first and carried his bat. His hundred was the first made for the new Essex club in county matches.

In 1894 only one first-class fixture was won in Essex's debut season as a first-class county, that being against Oxford University when Owen scored 109, Essex's first century that summer.

Owen took over the county captaincy from Alfred Lucas in 1895 and certainly brought a sense of fun to Essex cricket, leading them to third place in the County Championship in 1897. When he stepped down as captain, he was paid the warmest of tributes by Charles Green and received a gold watch and chain, scroll, gun and a purse of 200 guineas.

OXFORD UNIVERSITY

Essex's only win of the 1894 season came when a weakened Oxford University side was beaten by nine wickets at Leyton. Walter Mead took 13 wickets but the Essex hero was Hugh Owen who hit 109 and 86 not out. His hundred was the first century hit for Essex as a first-class county and their only three-figure score of the season.

In June 1922 Chelmsford staged its first first-class match when Oxford University were the visitors to what is now the County Ground. Jack Freeman had the honour of scoring the first century on the ground, 139 but the match ended in a draw.

Only ten players appeared for Essex in the 1962 match. Barry Stead was selected but failed to appear, opting to play instead for Nottinghamshire 2nd XI against Worcestershire 2nd XI at Halesowen.

P

PAKISTAN

When Essex beat the touring Pakistan team by nine wickets at Leyton in August 1962, they became the first county to have beaten all the major touring countries. Trevor Bailey (five for 47) and Barry Knight (four for 66) in Pakistan's first innings both went on to perform the double.

PEARCE, TOM

Tom Pearce had already scored his maiden first-class century, 152 against Lancashire when, in 1933, he took over the captaincy of Essex, sharing the duties with Denys Wilcox. The county finished in fourth place that summer, their highest position since 1897 and with more wins than ever before. In 1935 Pearce topped the 1,000 run mark for the first time, hitting the first of two centuries, 105 against Lancashire at Chelmsford, in the knowledge that his wife was undergoing an operation for appendicitis in the hospital overlooking the ground.

The following summer he was chosen for the Gentlemen v Players match at Lord's and in making 85, took his aggregate of first-class runs past 1,000. During the winter of 1938, he informed the Essex committee that he would be unable to captain the side in 1939, owing to business commitments.

After the war he was fortunately able to resume the captaincy. His experience, temperament and consistent batting were never more necessary than in those first few post-war seasons. He led the side from the front, scoring five centuries in his total of 1,332 runs whilst in 1947 he scored 1,597 runs at 45.62, hitting 137 not out and 96 against Worcestershire at New Road. Although the county had a disappointing season in 1948 Pearce scored 1,825 runs at an average of 49.32 and hit the highest score of his career, 211 not out against Leicestershire.

In 1949, Pearce's last season as captain, he was elected to the Test selection committee. As captain Pearce was always calm and good-natured and could bring the best out of a side. At the end of 1952 he became chairman of the Essex club, a position he held for 21 years. In 1961-62 he was manager of the MCC tour of India, Pakistan and Sri Lanka. He was also honorary team manager for the Scarborough Cricket Festival and in 1979 was deservedly awarded the OBE for his services to sport.

PERRIN, PERCY

Percy Perrin made his Essex debut in 1896 in the match against Surrey when he was two weeks short of his twentieth birthday. Facing Tom Richardson, Bill Lockwood and Tom Hayward, the young Perrin battled hard to score 52. Later that summer, he hit his maiden century, 139 against Warwickshire at Edgbaston. As a batsman, he could dominate any attack and was at his best against fast bowling, earning himself the title of 'the best batsman never to have played for England'.

In 1899 he was in fine form throughout the season and scored 1,491 runs including six centuries. Against Kent at Leyton in 1900, Perrin hit 205 before being caught in the deep. It was his first double hundred.

In 1903 he was credited with a hundred in three consecutive innings, including 170 and 102 not out in the match against Nottinghamshire at Trent Bridge. In the match against Derbyshire at Chesterfield in 1904, Perrin scored 343 not out from Essex's total of 597 in their first innings. He hit 68 fours, although it was said some years later that 14 of his boundaries would now be classed as sixes. Perrin's innings remains the only triple century ever made by an Essex player in county cricket but as unbelievable as it may seem, Essex lost.

In 1905, Perrin hit a hundred in each innings – 140 and 103 not out in the match against Middlesex at Lord's, the second coming against the clock to win the match for Essex. At the end of the season, he was chosen as one of *Wisden's* Five Cricketers of the Year. Perrin was the leading batsman again the following season when he scored 1,893 runs, which at the time was an Essex record.

Percy Perrin was always reliable as batsman, scoring more than 1,000 runs in 18 seasons. However, he could not field. He was heavy on his feet and could not move quickly to the ball. He certainly had a safe pair of hands and a long reach but his inability to move at great speed prevented him from ever appearing for his country.

After the First World War Perrin was aged forty-three but still had a few years of batting left in him. In 1919 he scored 126 and 101 not out against Kent at Leyton. He finished his active cricket career with 51 against Oxford University at Colchester in 1928, bringing his total of runs to 29,172 at an average of 36.19. He was by this time, fifty-two years of age and reappeared in the Essex side as captain, though he had practically retired three years earlier.

Perrin was elected to the Test selection committee, becoming its chairman in 1939. He was a real personality – spectators watching him with great admiration and interest. He maintained an active interest in cricket right up to his death at Hickling, Norfolk, in November 1945.

PHILLIP, NORBERT

Norbert Phillip had played cricket for both the Windward Islands and the Combined Islands since 1969 but he found it difficult to break into the West Indian Test team despite his obvious ability as a hard-hitting batsman and quick bowler.

Essex had tried to register Richard Hadlee for the second half of the 1977 season but when the TCCB would only sanction such action if a three-year contract was offered, the county turned their attentions to Norbert Phillip. It is generally accepted that Phillip himself made the first tentative approaches. He was obviously very keen to further his career, both in England and at Test level, and he arrived at Essex as a completely unknown player.

In 1978, his first season with the county, he helped to bring about a memorable victory at Gloucester, hitting a magnificent 134. It was a maiden century of awesome power. His hundred arrived in 112 minutes and contained seven sixes and 12 fours.

There were many occasions in his career with Essex when Phillip was to plunder the opposition attack. He launched an onslaught on the Northamptonshire bowlers in the Benson and Hedges Final of 1980 but could not quite snatch victory in the last over as he was at the non-striker's end for the majority of it.

Norbert Phillip represented the West Indies in nine Test matches with his best performances with both bat and ball coming against India, 47 and four for 48.

On the first day of the match against Surrey at Chelmsford in May 1983, play was washed out. On the second day, Essex totalled 287, leaving Surrey with just an hour to bat. They were dismissed for just 14 inside 15 overs with Norbert Phillip taking six for 4 off 7.3 overs. Later in the season he completed the first hat-trick of his career in the match against Northamptonshire at Wellingborough – yet he was only in the side because Derek Pringle had broken a finger.

Norbert Phillip was a good player and he played an important role in the first years of Essex's later success.

POINTS

Three times Essex finished with equal most points at the head of the John Player Sunday League before they won their first trophy in 1979. In 1989 they were docked 25 points for an unsatisfactory pitch at Southend. Worcestershire won the championship that year finishing six points ahead of Essex.

PRESTON, KEN

Discovered by Alf Gover, Ken Preston was given a trial by Essex towards the end of the 1947 season and, under the expert tuition of the former Surrey paceman, was able to increase his pace and master the art of swerve.

He was looked upon as a great prospect but then he broke his left leg playing football. It was a blow to both Essex and England, for he was coming into top form at a time when the national side were short of fast bowlers. Although he made a full recovery, he was never to bowl as quickly as he did in the summer of 1948.

By 1953 Ken Preston had shortened his run-up and it paid dividends as he took 91 wickets. The following season he developed a useful leg-cutter and this, coupled with far greater accuracy, resulted in him taking 94 wickets. He seemed to be improving every season and in 1955, crept even closer to the 100-wicket mark, taking 96 wickets at 23.19 runs apiece.

After injuries decimated his summer of 1956, he returned to County Championship action in 1957, taking 140 wickets at 20.35 runs each. The following summer he missed the 100 wicket mark by just one, claiming 99 wickets, but after that injuries forced him to miss parts of each of the next six seasons of county cricket.

A great servant of Essex cricket, having taken 1,155 wickets at 26.22 runs apiece, Ken Preston was widely respected in the game. He was also an extremely popular player and became the first secretary of the Essex Supporters' Club.

PRICHARD, PAUL

This Billericay-born batsman had an excellent first season with Essex in 1984, hitting 888 runs at 32.88 and scoring his maiden first-class century against Lancashire at Old Trafford. There followed another highly promising season before he topped the 1,000 run-mark in 1986 with 1,165 runs at 31.48 and a highest score of 147 not out against

Nottinghamshire at Chelmsford. That summer, Essex won the County Championship and there is no doubt that Prichard benefited greatly from Allan Border's presence, both on and off the field.

Injuries restricted his appearances in 1987 but the following summer, in spite of not reaching three figures, he again topped the 1,000 run-mark. After a disappointing 1989, Prichard bounced back to form in 1990, scoring 1,276 runs at 47.25 and hitting the highest score of his career – 245 against Leicestershire at Chelmsford, sharing in a new Essex record stand of 403 for the second wicket with Graham Gooch.

Paul Prichard.

He maintained his form the following season, scoring 1,031 runs at 36.82 as Essex won the County Championship and then again in 1992 he scored 1,399 runs at 43.71 as the county won the title for the second year in succession. Despite a disappointing finish in the County Championship in 1993,

Prichard again topped the 1,000 run-mark and scored another double hundred, 225 against Sussex at Hove.

He was appointed captain in 1995 and scored 1,000 runs for the seventh time as Essex finished fifth in the County Championship, a position he led them to again the following season. The pressures ceratinly did not affect his batting, for in 1997 he scored 1,098 runs at 45.75 with a top score of 224 against Kent at Canterbury.

After handing over the captaincy to Nasser Hussain, injuries have restricted his first team appearances but this loyal servant, who has scored 16,557 first-class runs at 34.85, remains an important member of the Essex squad.

PRINGLE, DEREK

The Nairobi-born son of Don Pringle, he shares a family record with the Armanaths and Hadlees in that his father played for East Africa in the 1975 World Cup but sadly he was killed in a car crash shortly afterwards.

Pringle impressed with the ball during his early years, taking all ten wickets when representing the Nairobi Schools Under-13 side. On moving to England, he attended the Felsted School and later Fitzwilliam College at Cambridge.

He made his Essex debut in 1978 and then gained his Blue the following summer when, as a freshman, he scored a century and took five wickets in the match against Oxford University.

His form at Cambridge was such that he was selected to make his Test debut for England in 1982, the last of his four summers at Fenners. His figures for Essex at this time were mediocre but he had performed exceptionally well with both bat and ball for Cambridge. In fact, to play in his second Test, he had to forego the honour of captaining the Light Blues at Lord's and let them beat Oxford University without him.

Pringle hit his maiden first-class hundred in the County Championship against Hampshire at Southend in 1983 and followed it with seven for 53 against Kent at Canterbury. He was developing into a highly intelligent all-rounder. In his University days he was a hard-hitting stroke player but then became more restricted, often sacrificing his personal achievements for his team's needs.

In 1985, he and Ken McEwan set a new Essex record for the third wicket in the John Player League with a stand of 190 against Warwickshire at Edgbaston, Pringle hitting an unbeaten 81. The following season he hit his highest score at Test level, 63 against India at Lord's, and in 1988 he hit the highest score of his first-class career – 128 against Kent at Chelmsford. He also produced his best bowling figures for England, five for 95 against the West Indies at Headingley.

In 1989 Pringle was the joint leading wicket taker, with Glamorgan's Steve Watkin, capturing 94 first-class wickets. It was a summer in which he produced his best figures with the ball, seven for 18 against Glamorgan.

Pringle continued to mature into a high class all-round cricketer but at the end of the 1993 season, after which he had scored 5,858 runs and taken 543 wickets, he left the game.

PROMOTION

Last summer Essex won promotion to the First Division of the County Championship after finishing the season as runners-up in Division Two to Northamptonshire.

Ronnie Irani and Stephen Peters launched a thrilling assault on the Warwickshire bowling at Chelmsford in Essex's last game of the season to clinch a promotion spot. Coming together with Essex in serious trouble at 64 for four in pursuit of 201, they destroyed the bowling with an unbroken partnership of 138. Essex reached their target with nearly 18 of their 56 overs to spare after their opponents, who also needed to win to gain one of the promotion places, had looked the more likely winners.

R

RECORD WICKET PARTNERSHIPS

The county's highest partnership for each wicket is as follows:

1st	316	G Gooch/P Prichard	v Kent at Chelmsford	1994
2nd	403	G Gooch/P Prichard	v Leicestershire at Chelmsford	1990
3rd	347*	M Waugh/N Hussain	v Lancashire at Ilford	1992
4th	314	S Malik/N Hussain	v Surrey at The Oval	1991
5th	316	N Hussain/M Garnham	v Leicestershire at Leicester	1991
6th	206	J Douglas/J O'Connor	v Gloucestershire at Cheltenham	1923
	206	B Knight/A Luckin	v Middlesex at Brentwood	1962
7th	261	J Douglas/J Freeman	v Lancashire at Leyton	1914
8th	263	D Wilcox/R Taylor	v Warwickshire at Southend	1946
9th	251	J Douglas/S Hare	v Derbyshire at Leyton	1921
10th	218	F Vigar/P Smith	v Derbyshire at Chesterfield	1947

REEVES, BILL

Bill Reeves was born at Cambridge, later joining the groundstaff at Leyton where his life was centred, for he married into the family of Edward Freeman, the Essex head groundsman who had played occasionally for the county.

He made his debut for Essex in 1897 and around the turn of the century he was given a greater role to play when he showed distinct promise as both a hard-hitting batsman and a right arm medium-pace bowler.

He strove hard to fill the gap left by Walter Mead's departure and in 1904 had his best season with the ball, taking 106 wickets at 16.16 runs apiece. The following season, Reeves produced his best form with the bat, hitting two centuries in his 1,174 runs with a highest score of 135 against Lancashire. Reeves hit his only other hundred for Essex in 1906. He scored 104 against Sussex as he and Claude Buckenham (68) put on 163 for the eighth wicket in only 70 minutes.

By 1909 he had recovered some of his lost form with the ball and took seven for 79 against Yorkshire at Leyton after hitting 71 out of a stand of 89 in just 45 minutes. In 1919 he and George Louden put on 122 for the last wicket in the match against Surrey and the following season, at the age of forty-five, he found something of his old zest, taking 62 wickets.

After scoring 6,451 runs and capturing 581 wickets for Essex, he became one of the best first-class umpires, standing in a number of Test matches.

REFUGE ASSURANCE CUP

After finishing third in the Refuge Assurance League of 1989, Essex qualified for the Refuge Assurance Cup semi-finals and their opponents were runners-up in the league, Warwickshire. After a resounding 101 run victory at New Road, Essex met Nottinghamshire in the final at Edgbaston and won a most exciting game and the cup, beating Nottinghamshire by five runs.

ROMFORD

Romford Cricket Club was founded in 1863 and used several grounds until 1944, when they applied to the council for the use of the sports ground and became co-tenants with the Gidea Park CC. Essex visited the ground for benefit matches several times but it was not until 1950 that a County Championship match was played there. The second match of the Romford week was against Worcestershire and Essex opener, Sonny Avery, took it for his benefit. The visitors scored 409, the highest score on the ground. On a subsequent visit they were bowled out for 76, the lowest score for a county side.

Trevor Bailey recorded the best bowling performance with eight for 49 and match figures of 14 for 81 when Hampshire were beaten there in 1957. He dominated the game, for in addition to his bowling he also made 59 and 71 not out from a total of 271 scored by Essex in both innings.

ROUND, JAMES

Educated at Eton College, James Round soon gained a reputation as a most effective long-stop and bowler of both fast round and slow under-hand. Moving on to Oxford University, he developed into the best amateur wicketkeeper of his day and represented the Gentlemen against the Players.He made four appearances for the Gentlemen, his most successful being that at the Oval in 1867 when he scored 29 and had a hand in the downfall of eight opponents. Also that year, he scored 142 for Southgate against Oxford University on the Magdalen Ground.

In 1868 he became a barrister and began his political career when he was elected MP for Colchester. He had been a member of the MCC since 1865 and served on the committee from 1869 to 1871.

Despite his parliamentary duties, he found an opportunity to devote a great deal of time to assist Essex in its formative years. He chaired the public meeting held at the Shire Hall, Chelmsford on 14 January 1876 and was chairman of the Essex club until 1882. In addition he was captain between 1876 and 1882.

James Round died at his home at Birch Hall on Christmas Eve 1916, aged seventy-four. His contribution to the game of cricket had been immense and he played an important part in driving Essex into the first-class game.

RUSSELL, JACK

The son of Tom Russell, who was for many years the Essex wicketkeeper, he made his county debut in 1908 but did not make his first half-century until 1911. Essex persevered with him and by 1913 Jack Russell's batting began to raise the highest hopes. His maiden first-class hundred came against Hampshire at Leyton when he hit 102 in helping Colin McIver put on 210 for the first wicket. In the last game of the season he hit a brilliant 110 against Lancashire at Old Trafford, thus becoming the only Essex batsman to reach 1,000 runs in county matches.

In 1914, against Leicestershire, he and McIver put on 212 for the first wicket – at the time a county record. He was the leading batsman in the first season after the war, scoring 1,387 runs including four centuries. It was not long after that his batting was noticed in quarters outside Essex and in 1920 he represented the Players against the Gentlemen, scoring 93 in the company of Hendren, Hobbs and Woolley. He was the first Essex player to pass 2,000 runs in a season and was rewarded with a place on the MCC tour to Australia in 1920-21 and he hit 135 not out at Adelaide in the third Test. The Australians followed England back to this country but Russell was not called upon until the fourth Test when he hit 101. He topped this in the next Test at the Oval with an unbeaten 102.

In that summer of 1921 Russell made the highest score of his career, 273 against Northamptonshire at Leyton, ending the season with 2,236 runs and second place to Philip Mead in the national averages.

His best year was 1922 when he put together an aggregate of 2,575 runs – the highest of all batsmen – including nine centuries for an average of 54.78. When Essex played Surrey at the Oval, Russell hit two separate hundreds in a match for the first time, scoring 115 and 118. He was named as one of *Wisden's* Five Cricketers of the Year and was selected for the MCC side to tour South Africa.

He was England's leading player in South Africa that winter, topping the Test averages with 436 runs at an average of 62.28. In the final Test, England batted first and scored 281 of which Russell made 140. South Africa were then dismissed for 179 but by this time, Russell had been forced to take to his bed. However, with England struggling at 26 for four, he returned to score 111 and help A E R Gilligan add 92 for the tenth wicket, a record in England v South Africa matches. He became the first Englishman to score two centuries in a Test and this feat has been commemorated in two ways – by a plaque in the Chelmsford pavilion and by the planting of a tree at the Kingsmead ground in Durban.

There can be few batsmen whose last three scores in Test matches were 96, 140 and 111 but Jack Russell was so ill on his return to England that Essex had to send him away on a recuperative holiday in the spring. He never played Test cricket again, his ten appearances bringing him 910 runs at an average of 56.87, including five centuries.

Once fully recovered, he continued scoring runs for Essex until 1930 when he retired, having scored 23,610 runs at 40.91, including centuries against every first-class county.

Following his retirement from first-class cricket, he was a coach and then a groundsman. He was also among those professional players granted honorary membership of the MCC, later standing as a first-class umpire for several seasons.

SCOREBOARDS

With the advent of one-day cricket, Essex created their famous mobile scoreboard. The first was made in 1962 from an old removal van adapted by the firm of J P Henisman. It was damaged by fire some nine years later and replaced by an articulated vehicle, converted by L and A Pinch of Hornchurch.

In 1981, an electronic scoreboard was erected at Chelmsford. This was given to the county by the contracting company, George Wimpey, to commemorate its centenary in Essex.

SEMI-FINALS

Up to the end of the 2000 season Essex had appeared in sixteen semi-finals of limited over competition, comprising six Gillette/Nat West Trophy matches, nine Benson and Hedges Cup games and one Refuge Assurance Cup match.

SMITH, PETER

It was in 1933 that Peter Smith, Essex's leading wicket taker, first took 100 wickets, a feat he was to achieve six times. That was also the year he suffered a cruel hoax. He was asked to report to the Oval, having been told that he had been selected to play for England against the West Indies.

When Essex defeated the Indian touring team at Brentwood in 1936, Peter Smith hit a century and shared 12 wickets with cousin Ray. He also put on 214 with Jim Cutmore for the eighth wicket in this match. In the following summer he was the country's leading wicket taker with 155 at 19.60 runs each. In 1938 he was chosen for the Gentlemen against the Players at Lord's and responded by taking nine wickets in the course of the game.

He was chosen for the MCC team to visit India in the winter of 1939-40 but, with the outbreak of war, this was cancelled. During the war years, he played some cricket against top-class opposition at Alexandria during his army service in the Middle East.

In 1946 he took 120 wickets at 19.49 runs each, backing this up with 834 runs and, but for absence through injury, would probably have completed the double that season. He took five wickets for one run in the space of 15 balls as Northamptonshire were bowled out for 106 after the first wicket had put on 96. In 1947, Peter Smith took 172 wickets – more than any Essex bowler had taken before – and produced his best figures of nine for 77 against Middlesex at Colchester. He also helped set another Essex batting record in the game against Derbyshire at Chesterfield. After complaining of feeling unwell, he came in at Number 11 to join Frank Vigar. They proceeded to put on 218 for the last wicket after Essex had been 199 for nine. Peter Smith scored 163, the highest score ever made by a Number 11 batsman. Not surprisingly he was chosen as one of *Wisden's* Five Cricketers of the Year.

During the winter months he became the only bowler ever to take nine wickets for the MCC in Australia when he took nine for 121 against New South Wales.

Smith, who took 1,610 wickets at 26.28 runs apiece, took three wickets in four balls on three occasions but failed to take a hat-trick. He was an extremely accurate bowler who could make the ball dip in flight and was more than capable of bowling out good batsmen on good wickets.

A great figure in the history of Essex cricket and a most popular player wherever he went, Peter Smith died from a brain haemorrhage following a fall when on holiday in France in 1967.

SMITH, RAY

Ray Smith was a dynamic batsman and a fast-medium bowler who could also revert to off-breaks when the occasion demanded.

During the Second World War he represented the British Empire XI and also captained an Essex XI against the British Empire XI at Chelmsford which raised almost £150 for King George's War Fund for Sailors.

In 1947, Ray Smith achieved the cricketer's double, scoring 1,386 runs and capturing 125 wickets, although he had the unenviable record of them being the most costly hundred wickets at 37.26 runs each. He scored 112 against Derbyshire at Colchester the following summer, reaching his maiden century in 63 minutes – the fastest hundred of the season. In 1949 he took 100 wickets for the fourth successive season and in 1950, which proved to be the worst season in the county's history, he performed the double, scoring 1,149 runs and capturing 102 wickets. When the South Africans visited Ilford in 1951, Smith hit the fastest hundred of the season. He was sent in early, reached his fifty in 40 minutes, his hundred in 70 minutes and was eventually dismissed for 147 in just 94 minutes – all this out of an Essex total of 204.

After doing the double again in 1952, scoring 1,045 runs and taking 136 wickets, it was disclosed that Ray Smith had received a three-year offer to play for Accrington in the Lancashire League. This prompted the Essex committee to offer him a three-year contract with a testimonial in the third year and a further three-year option if the county wanted to keep him.

Smith, whose last season was 1956, was a great club man and a fine cricketer, scoring 11,125 runs and taking 1,317 wickets but he was never to play for his country. Perhaps his attitude towards the county he played for can be summed up by his remark: 'I would give a month's salary if we could beat Yorkshire'.

SOMERSET

Founded in 1875, Somerset went 100 years without winning a trophy before they won five one-day titles – the Benson and Hedges Cup in 1981 and 1982, the 1979 Gillette Cup and Sunday League and the Nat West Trophy in 1983.

Somerset were Essex's opponents in the summer of 1895 when the county registered their first victory in the championship. Herbert Carpenter was the game's top scorer, his innings of 52 without a single boundary being of great importance as wickets tumbled around him. Yet in the return fixture at Taunton, Carpenter hit 153 at a run a minute before being run out. In this match, Charles McGahey scored 147 as Essex totalled 692 and went on to win by an innings and 317 runs.

The county's first match at Chelmsford in June 1926 resulted in the first tie in Essex's history, although the outcome was not determined until an appeal was made to the MCC. With less than a minute to play the scores were level. Eight wickets had been lost as Essex strove to score 138 for victory and Eastman, in attempting the winning hit, was caught by Earle. Last man, Ridley, raced from the pavilion but the umpires removed the bails and, although Somerset skipper John Daniell sportingly asked for the game to continue, play ended. The umpires then ruled that Somerset should be deemed to have won on first innings but Essex questioned the decision and referred the matter to the MCC who ruled that the match was a tie and the points should be shared.

The 1966 meeting at Ilford was an historic occasion – it was the first county match to include Sunday play. At that time clubs were not allowed to make an admission charge on a Sunday but £500 was paid by spectators for scorecards, stand seats and collections. It was an exciting finish with Essex being set 290 to win. With the score on 284 for seven, Robin Hobbs needed to hit the last ball for six to win. He could only manage two and the game was drawn.

In the match at Taunton in 1985, David East took eight catches behind the stumps in Somerset's first innings, thus equalling the world record held by Wally Grout of Australia.

SOUTH AFRICA

Essex's meeting with South Africa at Southend in 1935 was a personal triumph for the army bowler, John Stephenson, brought in to replace 'Hopper' Read who was being rested prior to the fifth Test. Stephenson took three of the first four wickets to fall for 11 runs and finished with seven for 66 as the tourists were dismissed for 250. Essex scored 302 in their first innings and then with Nichols and Stephenson, who had match figures of 10 for 110, bowling well, were left to make 172 for victory, which they did for the loss of only three wickets.

One of the most exciting matches against the South Africans was at Ilford in 1951. The tourists declared their first innings closed at 312 for nine but Essex passed that total, declaring their first innings at 319 for seven with Dickie Dodds scoring 138. South Africa scored 286 for five before declaring and setting Essex 280 to win in a little over two hours.

Ray Smith was sent in early and smashed the season's fastest hundred in just 70 minutes, finally being out for 147 as Essex ended on 255 for five, 25 runs short of their objective.

There were some good individual performances against the South Africans in 1960, with Insole scoring a century and Bailey taking seven for 81, but the tourists still won by six wickets.

SOUTHEND-ON-SEA

Southchurch Park, Southend-on-Sea has recently regained favour at the expense of Chalkwell Park, Westcliff-on-Sea because it can accommodate much larger crowds.

The first county match to be held here was in August 1906 when Leicestershire were the visitors. Essex won comfortably with Johnny Douglas taking eight for 33 in the second innings.

Perhaps the Southchurch ground's main claim to fame is the 721 runs scored in a single day by the Australians in 1948. With Bradman scoring 187 in a little over two hours and both Loxton and Saggers also hitting centuries, it was strange to see Keith Miller dismissed by Bailey for a duck.

One of the most recent records set on the ground was in 1983 when Essex totalled 310 for five against Glamorgan – a Sunday League record innings total – and Graham Gooch scored 176, which was a Sunday League individual innings record.

SUCH, PETER

Peter Such began his first-class career with Nottinghamshire in 1982, picking up 25 wickets at a cost of 29.48 and taking his first five-wicket haul, five for 112 against Gloucestershire. He still proved expensive the following summer but improved his best figures with six for 123 against Kent at Trent Bridge. In 1984 he finished second to Richard Hadlee in the Nottinghamshire bowling averages with 42 wickets at 22.30 runs apiece. After that he lost form and at the end of the following season, he joined Leicestershire.

Such struggled during his three seasons at Grace Road and joined

Essex for the start of the 1990 season. After appearing in only a handful of games in his first two seasons, he finished second in the Essex bowling averages in 1992 with 39 wickets at 22.94 and a new best of six for 17 against Sussex at Southend as the county won the championship title for the second year in succession.

Such formed a formidable spin bowling attack with John Childs and again finished second in the averages and won the first of eleven Test caps against Australia at Old Trafford where he took six for 77. In 1994, he took 51 wickets, including a then career best of seven for 66, against Hampshire at Southampton.

Such had his best season for Essex in 1995, taking 75 wickets at 25.86 with another devastating display of spin bowling against Hampshire at Colchester, where he took eight for 93. In 1996, he topped the county's bowling averages for the first time with 70 wickets at 27.34 and a return of eight

Peter Such.

for 118 against Yorkshire at Headingley. He was Essex's leading wicket taker the following season and has since been one of the county's most consistent performers, having taken 537 wickets at 29.03 runs apiece.

SUNDAY LEAGUE

The Sunday League was introduced in 1969 and Essex became particularly adept at the 40-over game, finishing third in the competition's inaugural season, fourth in 1970 and were the runners-up in 1971, missing the title by three-thousandth's of a run. The county came third in 1972 and fourth in 1975 before finishing runners-up again in 1976 and 1977, losing the title on a slower scoring rate in 1976.

Essex finally won the Sunday League title in 1981, their success being totally a team effort and not dependant on one or two key players. They had been fourteenth the previous season and so were, no doubt, surprising winners, finishing six points clear of Somerset and previous season's champions, Warwickshire.

Essex won the Sunday League title for a second time in 1984, a season when they were also crowned County Champions. Happily for them, none of their matches ended in 'No Result' whereas Sussex, who were third, had three. Essex's Sunday League records include:

Highest innings total	310 for five v Glamorgan at Southend	1983
Lowest innings total	69 v Derbyshire at Chesterfield	1974
Highest individual innings	176 by Graham Gooch v Glamorgan at Southend	1983
Best bowling performance	8 for 26 by Keith Boyce v Lancashire at Old Trafford	1971
Highest partnership	273 for second wicket (Graham Gooch and Ken McEwan v Nottinghamshire at Trent Bridge	1983
Most runs in a season	693 by Ken McEwan	1980
Most wickets in a season	33 by Keith Boyce	1971

SURREY

Founded in 1845, Surrey won three unofficial titles before capturing the first official County Championship in 1890. The county have won seventeen Championships altogether, including an unprecedented run of seven successive wins from 1952 to 1958.

Their last Championship success came in 2000. The county have also won all the one-day competitions, winning the Benson and Hedges Cup in 1974, the Nat West Trophy in 1982 and the Sunday League in 1996.

County Champions Surrey visited Leyton in August 1895 and by lunch on the first day had reached 129 for one. In the afternoon, a dynamic spell of fast bowling by Charles Kortright, who clean bowled six of Surrey's top order in the space of 15 balls at a cost of just four runs to finish with seven for 72, brought Essex back into the game but they eventually lost by 201 runs.

The strong Surrey side were beaten by an innings when they visited Leyton in 1896. Essex batted first and scored 327 but after that, the wicket began to crumble and Surrey were bowled out for 126 and 82.

In 1934, during the Brentwood cricket week, Essex beat Surrey by an innings and 192 runs with 'Hopper' Read having an outstanding match.

He removed Jack Hobbs's cap with his first ball and clean bowled him with his sixth. The new fast bowler ended with seven for 35 as the visitors were all out for 115. Essex amassed 570 for eight declared with Jack O'Connor making 248 and Claude Ashton 118. Surrey were then bowled out for 263, leaving Essex victorious inside two days.

At the Oval in 1946, Dickie Dodds and Sonny Avery established a record first wicket partnership of 270 – Dodds scoring 103 and Avery 210.

There was no play on the first day of the championship match at Chelmsford in May 1983 but Essex, put in to bat on day two, scored 287 with Keith Fletcher hitting a fine 110. Surrey were then bowled out for just 14 in 14.3 overs, the lowest score ever made against Essex, with Phillip taking six for 4 and Foster 4 for 10. Following on, a fine innings of 101 not out by Roger Knight helped the visitors draw the match.

SUSSEX

Founded in 1839, Sussex have seven times been County Championship runners-up but have never managed to win the title. They won the first two Gillette Cups and gained the trophy again in 1978, won the Sunday League in 1982 and the Nat West Trophy in 1986.

In the match at Leyton in 1927, Sussex captain Arthur Gilligan set Essex 276 to win in three-and-a-half hours. The home side won with 25 minutes to spare with Leonard Crawley hitting an unbeaten 176, including twice hitting Tate on to the roof of the pavilion as he and Hubert Ashton added the last 114 runs in an hour.

When the two counties again met at Leyton in 1933, Essex scored 561 for nine declared, a total in which no batsman scored a century and there were no partnerships of a hundred.

In 1982, in the Benson and Hedges Cup zonal match at Hove, Graham Gooch hit the Sussex attack for 198 not out. His innings, which contained five sixes and 22 fours, was the highest score made in any one-day competition in England.

T

TAYLOR, BRIAN

Having joined the Essex staff straight from school, Brian Taylor made his first-class debut in 1949 at the age of sixteen against Cambridge University at Fenners. After that he had to do his National Service and so the county signed Paul Gibb from Yorkshire.

In 1954 an injury to Gibb gave Taylor his first real chance in the senior eleven and he grasped it with both hands. As well as deputising capably as a wicketkeeper he showed such promise as a forcing left handed batsman that, after Gibb returned, Taylor often appeared in the Essex side by virtue of his batting abilities. It was not until 1956 that he became the county's regular keeper. He dismissed 75 batsmen and scored his maiden first-class century, 127 against Glamorgan at Cardiff in a total of 1,259 runs. Taylor was awarded his county cap and chosen by the Cricket Writers' Club as the Best Young Player of the Year and to top it all, he was selected to tour South Africa with the MCC under the leadership of Peter May.

In 1957, Taylor had another good season, scoring 1,311 runs and claiming 83 victims, yet he had eleven ducks. Two years later he had his best season with the bat, scoring 1,837 runs at an average of 30.61, and he hit the highest score of his career, 135 against Middlesex at Lord's.

Taylor broke Essex's record for the number of wicketkeeping dismissals in 1962 with 79 catches and 10 stumpings. Prior to the start of the 1967 season he was invited to lead Essex and, on acceptance, became the county's first professional captain.

'Tonker' Taylor hit the county's first century in the John Player Sunday League, taking 100 off 81 balls in 95 minutes against Derbyshire at Buxton. In July 1972 he was forced to miss Essex's match with Kent at Maidstone – only the first he had to miss since Essex met Middlesex at Lord's in 1961. At the end of the season, he was chosen as one of *Wisden's* Five Cricketers of the Year.

Brian Taylor.

In 1973, Taylor's last year in the Essex side, he had become a Test selector. Although he missed eight matches, he still passed Herbert Strudwick's record of 964 catches in County Championship matches. His total number of victims was 1,231– 1,040 caught and 191 stumped – and he remained active in cricket long after his first-class retirement, captaining Essex 2nd XI until 1981 and coaching Cambridge University from 1979 to 1985.

TIED MATCHES

Essex have been involved in five tied County Championship matches. The first was on the Chelmsford ground against Somerset in 1926. The visitors had secured a first innings lead of 30 but fine bowling from Eastman, who took six for 59, and Nichols, four for 45, dismissed them for 107 in their second innings. This left Essex requiring 138 runs to win. With eight wickets down, the scores were level with Perrin and Eastman at the wicket and barely a minute of play remaining. Eastman lashed out in the hope of making the winning hit but was caught at mid-off. As the last Essex man, Ridley ran out, umpire Frank Chester pulled up the stumps, his ruling being that as Somerset led on the first innings, they were entitled to the three points for first innings lead and Essex to merely one point. A request was sent to the MCC for a ruling and the decision was that the match was a tie, with the points to be divided equally.

Essex's match against Northamptonshire at Ilford in 1947 also ended in a tie. The visitors scored 215 before Chick Cray, opening with Sonny Avery, made 100 in an Essex total of 267. When Northants went in again, Jackie Timms played a magnificent innings of 112 which overshadowed Cray's maiden hundred. Northants reached 291, leaving Essex to get 240 in five hours. Cray went quickly this time, but a fourth wicket stand of 103 by Vigar and Clark put Essex on their way. Wickets then began to fall steadily and, as wicketkeeper Tom Wade walked out to join his captain Tom Pearce, 11 runs were wanted in a little over a quarter-of-an-hour. Wade promptly hit a four and a procession of singles brought the scores level but with only two minutes remaining, Clarke yorked Wade.

Four years later, Essex entertained Lancashire at Brentwood. After Alan Wharton (85) and Winston Place (63) had given Lancashire a good start, Ken Preston and Ray Smith sent the last six men back for 29 runs and the red rose county were all out for 266. It looked a big score when Essex had eight down for 187 but a ninth wicket stand of 72 between Bill Greensmith and Frank Vigar got Essex to within five runs of the Lancashire score. Lancashire then made 226 for seven before declaring to leave Essex 140 minutes to score 232. Ray Smith followed up his 11 wickets in the match with a hard hit 48 but though the runs came quickly, so did the loss of wickets and at 206 for nine, it seemed like Lancashire's match. The last over arrived with Bailey at the crease and nine runs needed for victory. Bailey hit the first ball for six and then collected two off the second ball to level the scores. After blocking the third, he made contact with the fourth delivery only to see Lancashire captain Nigel Howard take a remarkable catch at full stretch.

Essex's fourth tied match was against Gloucestershire at Leyton in 1959 and was Ken Preston's benefit game. Unfortunately he had an injured arm and could not play. On a beautiful batting track, Essex made 364 for six before declaring with Doug Insole scoring 177 not out. Arthur Milton, who was leading the western county in the absence of Emmett and Graveney, failed by one run to record his seventh hundred of the summer as Gloucestershire totalled 329.

As Essex went in search of quick runs, Insole made 90, allowing them to declare at 176 for eight. Gloucestershire had ten minutes short of three hours in which to score 212 for victory. From being 131 for eight and needing another 81 runs, Gloucestershire, thanks to a whirl-wind innings by Tony Brown, shot to 209 before Bailey claimed his wicket. After Bailey had bowled a wide, Meyer scampered a single to level the scores. Barry Knight, who was awarded his county cap after this match, bowled at the other end and had Sam Cook caught by the South African Milner who dived forward from his position at short-leg to take a superb catch.

Essex's record fifth tied match came against Sussex at Hove in 1974. The home side batted first and scored 245 on a wicket that always gave the bowler a little help. Essex declared their first innings closed at 200 for eight and Sussex entered into the spirit of the game by scoring 173 for five before they, too, declared their innings. Needing 219 for victory, Essex lost their tenth and final wicket with the scores level.

TURNER, STUART

Chester-born all-rounder Stuart Turner made his Essex debut in 1965 but was released before being recalled two seasons later. In 1968 he hit his maiden first-class century against Glamorgan at Ilford, helping Robin Hobbs add 192 for the eighth wicket in just under two hours. In 1970, coming in at 67 for six in the match against Somerset at Taunton, Turner hit 121 out of 163 in three hours, the highest score of his career. It was during this season that Turner won a regular place in the side for the first time, his brisk medium-pace bowling bringing him 65 championship wickets and his county cap.

In the opening match of the 1971 season, he performed the hat-trick against Surrey, his victims being Storey, Long and Jackman.

In 1974, in the match against Glamorgan at Swansea, Essex were 202 for nine when Acfield joined Turner who was on 31. They stayed together for 133 minutes and 42 overs, adding 122 for the last wicket with Turner finishing on 118 not out. He ended the summer with 963 runs and 73 wickets, winning the Wetherell Award as the country's leading all-rounder, emulating Keith Boyce's feat. Turner also came close to selection for the England tour to Australia, being high in the selector's minds. He was certainly unlucky not to have gained representative honours of some sort because of his natural all-round ability.

In 1977, his haul of 77 first-class wickets included his career best figures of six for 26 against Northamptonshire. During the course of the 1979 season Turner hit 102 in 110 minutes in the match against Kent, and took ten wickets, including five for 5, for the only time in his career against Northamptonshire.

In one-day cricket, his nagging accuracy and selective hitting and ability in the field, made him invaluable. In 1986 at Southchurch Park, Southend, Stuart Turner received a plaque from the Association of Cricket Statisticians to commemorate his achievement on becoming the first player to score 3,000 runs and take 300 wickets in the John Player League. He had been one of Brian Taylor's 'magnificent twelve' and yet in his early days at county level he had been told that he was not good enough. He went on to play for twenty years, scoring 9,264 runs and taking 810 wickets, proving those early critics wrong.

TWO THOUSAND RUNS

The first batsman to notch up 2,000 runs in a season for Essex was Jack Russell in 1920 when he scored 2,042 runs at 45.37. The highest number of runs scored in any one season for the county is Graham Gooch's 2,559 at 67.34 in 1984. The full list of Essex players scoring 2,000 runs in county matches in a season is:

Batsman	Runs	Average	Year
Graham Gooch	2,559	67.34	1984
Jack O'Connor	2,308	56.29	1934
Jack O'Connor	2,256	48.00	1928
Jack Russell	2,243	53.40	1922
Jack O'Connor	2,224	48.34	1929
Ken McEwan	2,176	64.00	1983
Doug Insole	2,142	47.60	1955
Jack O'Connor	2,077	44.19	1933
Jack Russell	2,062	66.51	1928
Jack Russell	2,042	45.37	1920
Mark Waugh	2,009	77.26	1990

U

UMPIRES

Bill Reeves, who became an umpire after taking 581 first-class wickets for Essex, told Yorkshire opening bowler George Macaulay: 'There's only one man who made more appeals than you, George, and that was Dr Barnardo.' Stan Nichols, during the Yorkshire v Essex match at Colchester in 1935, hit a ball for six. It was declared void when the umpires realised that there was no batsman at the other end, a wicket having fallen the previous ball.

For many years, umpires were not allowed to officiate in matches involving their own county but Frank Chester, with permission from the captains, stood in the Worcestershire v Essex match of 1925 when West had to leave suddenly due to a death in the family.

V

VICTORIA

Essex, the English county champions, met Australia's Sheffield Shield premiers, Victoria, at Chelmsford in September 1991. This first Anglo-Australian challenge produced some absorbing cricket and a thunderstorm at lunchtime on the fourth and final day saved Victoria from an innings defeat. If Essex were weary after a long season, it hardly showed. Nor did Victoria's inevitable winter rustiness, thanks to a few warm-up games.

Essex were 199 for five at the end of the first day, an innings not concluded until the third day, after rain permitted only an hour's play on the Tuesday. Gooch declared at 343 for nine with Pringle, Stephenson and Knight all scoring half centuries. Then Childs and Such spun the ball viciously to reduce Victoria to 71 for six before Merv Hughes and Tony Dodemaide steadied the innings. Foster dropped Hughes at mid-wicket allowing him to finish 60 not out in Victoria's first innings total of 168.

Following on, Victoria had collapsed to 56 for eight when a Melbourne-type cloudburst cheated Essex of the £12,000 winners' money.

VICTORIES

Essex's greatest number of victories in a County Championship season is 13 from 22 matches in 1979 when the county won the title, finishing 77 points clear of runners-up Worcestershire. Their biggest victory came in 1895 when they beat Somerset at Taunton by an innings and 317 runs.

VIGAR, FRANK

Tall, ungainly, yet very determined, Frank Vigar was a right-handed batsman and leg-break bowler. He hit his maiden first-class century against Gloucestershire at Chalkwell Park, Westcliff in 1939. Sent in as nightwatchman to save the wicket of Jack O'Connor, he went on the next day to score 121 and save Essex from following on. O'Connor was dismissed by the first ball he faced the next morning.

After the war Vigar made a confident start to first-class cricket and in 1947 hit 1,735 runs, including five centuries. In the match against Derbyshire at Chesterfield, he and Peter Smith set a new record for the Essex tenth wicket. When Smith joined Vigar, the Essex total stood at 199 for nine. They put on 218, Peter Smith hitting 163, the highest score ever made by a Number 11 batsman, and Frank Vigar scored 114 not out.

Probably the unhappiest moment of Vigar's career came in the match against the Australians at Southend in 1948. Tom Pearce brought him on to employ his gentle leg-spin for the last over before lunch in an attempt to lure Don Bradman into a reckless stroke. In fact not a single ball of the over touched the ground, the Don simply went down the track and cracked the first five balls over the boundary and the sixth extremely hard to mid-off. To cap it all, Frank Vigar suffered a pair.

A useful all-rounder, Vigar went on to score 8,660 runs and take 236 wickets before, at the end of the 1954 season, the Essex committee decided to terminate his engagement.

W

WADE, TOMMY

Tommy Wade began his career as an off-break bowler, taking four for 11 against Nottinghamshire at Colchester and then five for 64 at Chelmsford in the match against Somerset. Also at Chelmsford, he and Roy Sheffield put on 110 for the last wicket against Warwickshire. It was Sheffield whom Tommy Wade was to replace as wicketkeeper in 1938. Prior to that, Wade was involved in another profitable last wicket stand as he and Ken Farnes added 149 in the match against Somerset at Taunton in 1936.

During the MCC tour of Australia in 1936-37, Wade kept wicket in two matches when both regular wicketkeepers, Les Ames and George Duckworth, were injured. He just happened to be visiting Australia at the time and was awarded an MCC touring cap for his appearances.

By 1938 he was Essex's regular wicketkeeper. It was to be his best season behind the stumps as he claimed 78 victims, 62 of them caught and 16 stumped. In the match against Kent at Colchester, he conceded just two byes out of the visitors' total of 742 and the first of those did not appear until the score had reached 626.

In 1947 Wade had 76 victims with exactly half that number being stumped. Towards the end of the 1948 season, however, he developed fibrositis and had a prolonged absence from the side as a result. His popularity was shown by the public response to his benefit. He netted more than £3,000, which was a record for an Essex professional.

At the end of the 1950 season, Tommy Wade, who had claimed 590 victims in his career, 413 caught and 177 stumped, decided to retire. He was a large man and known for his shriek-like appeal on the field of play and as a practical joker off duty.

WARTIME

War was declared on 4 August 1914 but first-class cricket continued almost unaffected through to the end of that month and the season although Surrey had to play their remaining home games at Lord's as the Oval was occupied by the army. When the 'it will all be over by Christmas' prophecy proved wrong there was no further thought of organised cricket but attempts were made by a number of counties to keep the game going and at Leyton a regular programme of matches against schools, clubs and Service sides was maintained. Three Essex players, Douglas, Gillingham and McIver, appeared in charity matches arranged at Lord's and in matches against Australian and Dominion forces' elevens.

During the Second World War the game was not abandoned totally and every year the public was entertained by matches of a high standard. They were usually one-day games and played at weekends. As the war progressed, Services cricket became better organised and regular matches were arranged between the Army, Royal Navy, RAF, Civil Defence, the National Fire Service and National Police teams.

Several counties were able to organise teams to play their closest neighbours but for a variety of reasons Essex was not one of them. It was in one of the areas of the country most vulnerable to attack and for long periods many of its grounds were in prohibited areas. In one respect, however, Essex remained represented in competitive cricket, playing in the annual match which took place at Lord's between Middlesex and Essex, Kent and Surrey.

The cricketing public in the south of England owed much, particularly in the early years of the war, to the British Empire XI and the London Counties. The contributions of Essex to the British Empire XI were many, with all-rounder Ray Smith often captaining the side. He scored 2,155 runs and captured 308 wickets for the British Empire XI during hostilities. Captain of the London Counties side was Lawrie Eastman, who was in charge in their first appearance at Lord's. Their leading batsman, until his appointment as coach at Eton in 1943, was Jack O'Connor. The departure of many leading professionals to league cricket in the north of England considerably weakened the Counties side in the later years of the war.

WARWICKSHIRE

Founded in 1882, Warwickshire have won the County Championship five times, in 1911, 1951, 1972, 1994 and 1995. The county also won the Gillette Cup in 1966 and 1968, the Nat West Trophy in 1989, 1993 and

1995 and the Benson and Hedges Cup in 1994. They also took the Sunday League title in 1980, 1994 and 1997.

Essex's opening County Championship match in 1895 was against Warwickshire at Edgbaston. They totalled 410 with both Higgins and Burns hitting centuries, the county's first in the competition. Kortright then took eight for 94 as Warwickshire were bowled out for 259. Warwickshire followed on but the match ended in a draw with the home side on 344 for five.

In 1950, Essex's match against Warwickshire at Ilford was the first to be televised by the BBC.

In 1974, Essex's West Indian Test all-rounder, Keith Boyce, performed the hat-trick against Warwickshire, his victims being Neil Abberley, Deryck Murray and Mike Smith. On the opening day of Ilford week in July 1984, Warwickshire made 334 with Alvin Kallicharran hitting a fine century. Essex were dismissed for 114 and forced to follow on. In their second innings, McEwan hit 97 and Gladwin 92 as Essex reached 374, leaving Warwickshire 56 overs to score 155 for victory. John Lever quickly removed Andy Lloyd and first innings centurion, Kallicharran, before Paul Smith and Dennis Amiss steadied the ship. Acfield then removed both batsmen in successive overs before Lever returned to pick up the wickets of Asif Din and Chris Old. Though Geoff Humpage hit some lusty blows, Derek Pringle took the last four wickets to give Essex an amazing victory by 35 runs.

WAUGH, MARK

The twin of Australian captain Steve Waugh, he scored heavily for New South Wales before joining Essex for the latter part of the 1988 season. Next season he was the county's leading run getter with 1,288 runs and a top score of 165 against Leicestershire at Grace Road. In 1990 he scored 2,009 runs for Essex at an average of 77.26 and hit his first double hundred for the county, 207 not out, against Yorkshire at Middlesbrough.

It was this kind of form that led to him making his Test debut against England at Adelaide in 1990-91. He showed his selection was long overdue by making a magnificent 138 after having replaced his brother in the team. While not as good a bowler as his brother Steve, he has performed well for Australia in one-day internationals and is a brilliant fieldsman. Also that season he scored 229 not out for New South Wales against Western Australia at Perth, sharing in an unbroken fifth wicket stand of 464 with his brother, Steve.

Waugh returned to Essex in 1992, scoring 1,253 runs at 78.31 and hitting his highest score for the county – a highly entertaining unbeaten 219 against Lancashire at Ilford – in which he and Nasser Hussain shared an Essex third wicket unbeaten stand of 347.

Mark Waugh.

During the 1993 Ashes tour, Waugh hit 137 and 62 not out in the fifth Test at Edgbaston. It won him the Man-of-the-Match award and led Australia to yet another victory.

In 1995 he returned to Essex for the last time, finishing second to Nasser Hussain in the county's batting averages with 1,347 runs at 51.80.

Mark Waugh has such ability that he can make batting look the easiest thing in the world and it is hard to imagine that he will not be a major force in Test cricket during the years ahead.

WEATHER CONDITIONS

Play was suspended in Essex's match against Cambridge University in April 1981 because it was too cold. The Essex match against Derbyshire rain prevented any play on the first two days, the game was transferred to the Garrison Ground in the same town.

·WESTCLIFF-ON-SEA

In 1933 Essex left their home at Leyton and, in looking for other grounds, settled for an appearance at Westcliff-on-Sea. There, in Chalkwell Park, they set up their seating beneath the trees in a corner of the ground that was normally used by two local clubs.

In 1936 the spinning fingers of Hedley Verity wrought havoc in the Essex ranks when he captured nine for 48 followed by another six to give him match figures of 15 for 100. Essex suffered again the following year when Johnny Clay took nine for 59 in the game against Glamorgan. But they were not always on the receiving end and Tom Pearce, that lusty-hitting Essex captain, took 211 from the Leicestershire attack in 1948.

WEST INDIES

During the summer of 1906, one of New Zealand's first great players, Daniel Reese, made his county debut for Essex. His best performance of the season came in the county's first victory over the West Indies at Leyton when he top-scored with 70 on a bowler's wicket.

In June 1922 Essex allocated a game to Valentine's Park, Ilford, for the first time. Their opponents were the West Indies, who had not yet received Test status but proved to be too good for a weakened Essex side which lost by three wickets.

WICKETKEEPERS

David East equalled Wally Grout's world record of eight dismissals in an innings when he took eight catches out of the nine Somerset wickets to fall at Taunton in 1985. Brian Taylor holds the record for the most dismissals in a season for Essex with his 1962 figures of 89. Of this total 79 were caught and 10 stumped.

The following wicketkeepers have made the most dismissals in county matches for Essex:

	Played	Matches	Caught	Stumped	Total
Brian Taylor	1949-73	539	1040	191	1,231
Tommy Wade	1929-50	318	413	177	590
David East	1981-89	185	480	53	533
Neil Smith	1973-81	178	381	47	428
Tom Russell	1894-05	162	246	88	334
Paul Gibb	1951-56	145	263	63	326
James Sheffield	1929-36	177	177	54	231
John Freeman	1905-28	336	163	46	209
Alfred Russell	1898-10	130	160	44	204
Richard Rollins	1992-99	67	152	21	173

WISDEN CRICKETER OF THE YEAR

The following Essex players have been selected as one of *Wisden's* Five Cricketers of the Year:

Frederick Bull	1898	Doug Insole	1956
Charles McGahey	1902	Brian Taylor	1972
Walter Mead	1904	Keith Boyce	1974
Percy Perrin	1905	Keith Fletcher	1974
Johnny Douglas	1915	Ken McEwan	1978
Hubert Ashton	1922	John Lever	1979
Jack Russell	1923	Graham Gooch	1980
Stan Nichols	1934	John Childs	1987
Ken Farnes	1939	Neil Foster	1988
Peter Smith	1947	Mark Waugh	1991
Trevor Bailey	1950	Stuart Law	1998

WORCESTERSHIRE

Founded in 1865, Worcestershire waited 99 years for their first title, winning the County Championship in 1964. They won it again in their centenary year, and in 1974, before winning it in successive years – 1988 and 1989. They have won the Sunday League on three occasions, 1971, 1987 and 1988; the Benson and Hedges Cup in 1991; and the Nat West Trophy in 1994.

Worcestershire were Essex's opponents in the first first-class match played at Castle Park, Colchester in 1914, a match Essex won by 193 runs.

In 1921, Essex beat Worcestershire by 132 runs despite trailing by 155 runs on the first innings. The victory was due almost entirely to Johnny Douglas and Jack Russell who, in Essex's second innings total of 500 for five declared, scored 123 not out and 151 respectively. Douglas also had match figures of 14 for 156. Jack O'Connor performed the hat-trick at Worcester in 1925, his leg-breaks bowling M K and H K Foster and then giving him a return catch off the bat of Gilbert Ashton. One of the closest finishes came in 1947 when Essex won by one wicket after being 111 on the first innings. Tommy Wade hit two boundaries in the last minute of the extra half-hour.

Y

YORKSHIRE

Founded in 1863, Yorkshire won two unofficial county titles in 1867 and 1870 before going on to take the record number of twenty-nine official championships, including a sequence of four successive titles between 1922 and 1925. But the once proud county has not tasted championship victory since 1968 when, having won six of the last nine championships, they were led by Brian Close. The strong side of the 1960s won the Gillette Cup in 1966 and 1969 but until 1987 when they won the Benson and Hedges Cup, their only title came in 1983 when they won the Sunday League.

The 1897 season saw Essex record a rare double of victories over Yorkshire. In the first meeting at Leyton Yorkshire were bowled out for 154 and Essex, thanks to Perrin and Russell, totalled 199. Kortright and Bull continued to hold the upper hand and the white rose county were dismissed for just 176 in their second innings, leaving Essex 132 to win. At 53 for five, it looked as though Yorkshire would be the victors but Mead and Kortright saw Essex home by three wickets.

In the return at Huddersfield Essex, batting first, were bowled out for 139, but with Kortright bowling at his fastest they had a lead of five runs on the first innings. Arthur Turner scored his maiden century as Essex left Yorkshire needing 299 to win. It was a stern task but the Yorkshire batsmen all made worthwhile contributions. As the last pair came together, 11 runs were still required, but with only one run needed for a tie, last man Bairstow was adjudged leg before.

Johnny Douglas who was destined to become a great force in Essex cricket made his first-class debut against Yorkshire in 1901, being bowled by Hirst for nought in both innings. Four years later, Douglas took five Yorkshire wickets in eight balls including the first hat-trick by an Essex player in first-class cricket. In future years, Yorkshire always seemed to bring the best out of Douglas as though he was trying to make amends for that pair in his first match.

At Leyton in 1932, Herbert Sutcliffe and Percy Holmes achieved a record 555 opening stand for Yorkshire against Essex. Yorkshire declared when that score was achieved but it was later discovered that the scoreboard was wrong, the official scorers claiming that the total was 554. Essex captain Charles Bray readily agreed to an extra run being found to enable the record to stand, although the matter has remained the subject of continuing controversy.

In 1935 Essex were capable of beating anyone, as they showed when they met Yorkshire at Huddersfield. After three years of being on the receiving end of Yorkshire's record opening stand, they bowled them out for just 31 runs – at one stage they were 9 for six – and 99. Stan Nichols had a superb match, taking 11 for 54 and making 146 out of Essex's total of 334. The story is told of the Yorkshire committee man who arrived a little late on the first day and asked the gateman for the score.

'Thirty for nine' came the reply.

'Thirty for nine, eh?' replied the committee man. 'Champion, champion. How many wickets has Bowes got?'

'Bowes?' came the gateman's retort. 'Bloody Bowes is batting.'

YOUNG CRICKETER OF THE YEAR

The annual award made by the Cricket Writers' Club, which was founded in 1946, is currently restricted to players qualified for England and under the age of twenty-three on 1 April. Three Essex players have been selected and they are:

1956	Brian Taylor
1983	Neil Foster
1989	Nasser Hussain

YOUNG, HARDING

Harding Young achieved early prominence in minor cricket while serving in the Royal Navy. The excellence of his bowling attracted the attention of Charles Green who had captained Essex between 1883 and 1888. He must have been greatly impressed, for he bought Young out of the Senior

Service to play for Essex. From this originated his nickname 'Sailor' by which he was known throughout the cricket world.

In 1899, his second season in the Essex side, Young took 139 wickets at a cost of 21.79 runs apiece including a career best eight for 54 against Warwickshire at Edgbaston. When Essex entertained the touring Australians at Leyton, they gained one of their greatest victories. 'Sailor' Young played his part to the full. After helping to add 55 for the last wicket in Essex's first innings total of 199, he took four for 42 as Australia were dismissed for 144. Essex, too, struggled and the Australians were left to make 200 to win. The Australians were bowled out for 73 with Young taking seven for 32. Also that summer, he played in two Test matches against Australia with his best figures being four for 30 in the match at Headingley.

'Sailor' Young dismissed ten or more batsmen in a match on three occasions and in 1907 he performed the only hat-trick of his career against Leicestershire at Leyton. Sadly, he suffered from muscular rheumatism and was unable to play regularly although he did tour the West Indies in 1910-11. He was on the ground staff at Lord's for a long time and often turned out for the MCC. From 1921 to 1931 he served as a first-class umpire and then, until a very late age, he was engaged in coaching schoolboys.

Z

ZENITH

Although Essex won the County Championship in successive seasons in 1983 and 1984 few of the county's fans will argue over which moment has been the finest in the club's history. In 1979 Essex not only won the County Championship for the first time, finishing 77 points ahead of second placed Worcestershire, but also beat Surrey in the final of the Benson and Hedges Cup.